BEYOND ME

Becoming a Follower of Jesus
Who Leads Others to Follow Jesus

Troy J Andreasen

Table of Contents

Preface

Where did this book come from?

This book came from a question I wrestled with for a long time…
Why do I find Christian discipleship so elusive to apply in the real world?
What does it even mean to be a "disciple?"

The concept of *biblical* discipleship is quite simple. It's apprenticeship. Francis Chan's book title describes it well… *Multiply: Disciples Making Disciples*.[1]

So then, if the idea is so simple, why do we see so *few* examples of this being lived out?

Of course, it doesn't happen by accident. We need to be intentional. We need to have a plan. But that's just the thing… There's no shortage of "discipleship" materials out there. Some of them are *excellent* resources (such as *Multiply*). And of course the goal of all those materials is to be applied! Yet I can read a bookcase full of discipleship books and study guides, but that doesn't automatically turn me into an active disciple who disciples.

Why is that?

One reason lines up with an idea from Kyle Idleman's book, *AHA*. He said that sometimes "we trick ourselves into believing that because we *feel* different, we're actually *doing* something different… We mistake our conviction for real change."[2] This is very true! Even given the *ideal* discipleship plan, we still need to actually *implement it*, and not just feel good about the ideas we learned.

Another reason we don't see more live examples of disciples making disciples is that it seems like there are some gaps in the existing resources. Even though I've learned much from some really good curricula, there tend to be some common areas of shortcoming or imbalance among the materials I've encountered.

- Much of the "discipleship" curricula is way more focused on *becoming* a disciple *myself* (i.e. a "student") than on *making* disciples of *others* (i.e. an "apprentice" who in turn apprentices others).

- Much of the material focuses on *either* leading people to Christ, or helping them mature in Christ; but few cover both.

- The strategies tend to be very polarized: either highly structured ("you need to cover exactly these things in this way"), or completely freeform ("just do life together and share what you know"). Personally, I love the idea of just "doing life together!" Yet in practice, if I don't have a plan, my natural *tendency* is to just hang out together socially. So why not a discipleship *plan* with *flexibility* and a vision that takes us beyond the material?

- Of the material intentional about *multiplying* disciples, there are not many practical tools for *ongoing* implementation: They either focus heavily on the *theory* of why "disciples making disciples" is a good idea, or they provide tools that the average Christian isn't equipped to *keep implementing* once they finish the curriculum.

As these frustrations built up over time, I felt more and more compelled by God to develop a discipleship plan that addresses these issues. A lot of people before me have paved the way with some great discipleship concepts. The goal of this curriculum is to assemble those ideas (and some new ones) into a plan that is highly geared toward *equipping* those coming to Christ today. A plan they can *apply*, *repeat*, and even *continue beyond* the scope of this material. This plan is designed to *disciple Christians* to both *outreach* to non-Christians and *disciple* newer Christians. My prayer is that this will be a step in the right direction toward that "ideal" introductory discipleship plan.

— Troy J Andreasen

1 Francis Chan and Mark Beuving, *Multiply: Disciples Making Disciples* (Colorado Springs, CO; David C Cook, 2012).
2 Kyle Idleman, *AHA: Awakening. Honesty. Action.* (USA; David C Cook, 2014) 148.

INTRODUCTION

Who is This Material For?

This material is for followers of Jesus. It's for people who *are* (or *desire to be*) *disciples* of Jesus. Not just studiers, not just fans, but people who want to _follow Jesus_. This material is designed to help brand *new* Christians mature with an outward focus. It's designed to help *not-so-new* Christians be equipped to *disciple others*. The material is a framework to ask the Holy Spirit to empower us to grow in these (and future) areas. Lessons 1 & 2 and Appendix B could be especially helpful to those who are *considering* a commitment to Jesus, or aren't *fully sure* whether or not they've understood and responded to God's gracious offer. (Those three lessons could even be used as a preview or sample of the curriculum.)

This material is for leaders who've been led through it. There needs to be a pioneer within your region or circle of ministry, of course. But this plan will be most effective if each of the new disciplers has been led through the curriculum themselves (at least a few weeks' head start). That way, even after a few steps in, they can implement 360° discipleship.

This material is recommended for groups of 2-4 people (including the discipler). Since the goal of this plan is to be *implemented* (not just learned), it's ideal for the leader to choose 1-3 other people to journey through the lessons with. We can't make disciples without involving other people, so *bring others* on this trek! But some of us may ask, "If I'm supposed to bring others, then why not include a whole bunch of people at the same time?" The larger a "small group" gets, the easier it becomes for the participants to simply be *recipients* rather than *apprentices*. It also gets a lot more complicated to line up schedules with a larger group. So a small group of 2-4 total gives the leader the best environment to help each member apply the material.

Group Covenant

Whether you experience this plan in a one-on-one environment, or in a group of 3-4, here are some basic principles we should agree to.

SAFETY — Each member of the group (including the leader) needs to have the confidence to share the *real* questions and *real* struggles they have, knowing the group will walk them through it with care and confidentiality.

COMMITMENT — For this plan to be effective, members need to *know that their team will be there for them*. This *starts with* the group meetings (but doesn't end there). So block your group meetings off on your calendar. *If you make excuses about simply showing up, you'll certainly make excuses about applying the plan*. So commit to your team.

BALANCED PARTICIPATION — Be mindful of encouraging (and allowing) all members to share. Don't rush to the next question too quickly because of being uncomfortable with a little silence. (Some people need more time to collect their thoughts and respond than others.) At the other end, don't let people get away with monopolizing the discussion parts. The nature of this group calls for everyone's participation.

ACCOUNTABILITY — The goal of accountability is not to make people feel guilty, but to care enough to help one another past our obstacles to godly change.

FUN — Having fun together is a great way to build community and help let our guards down. Some leaders will need to avoid the temptation to be all business, all the time in their group. Others will need to avoid the temptation to be all fun, all the time. Journey through the material together, but make sure you enjoy the trip.

DO LIFE TOGETHER — There's much you can learn from one another, and ways to sharpen one another, and enjoy time together — beyond this material. The best groups will develop a friendship beyond their official meetings. Hang out together. Run errands with someone from the group. Lend a hand. Share life skills. Have life talks.

FLEXIBILITY — Real life is messy. Allow room for God-tangents. The Holy Spirit might lead in a direction that's not in the book. Or maybe a member of the group needs extra care a certain week to process something big that's going on in their life. That's okay. Go with it. That might mean setting aside extra time for your meeting, or putting the lesson on pause and coming back to it the next week. Or, if there's more you want to cover deeply than your time allows for, put it on pause and continue with it next time. Remember, the goal is discipleship, not just rushing through the material.

Likewise, the curriculum doesn't need to fit neatly into a semester or consecutive 12 weeks. The best timing to *start* going through this material with someone new *may* be in the middle of a semester. You don't even need to complete it on the "disciplee" end before starting it with someone new on the discip*ler* end. (Though at least a few weeks into it would be helpful.) If you reach the end of a semester before the end of the material (or someone moves away, etc), set up a plan for how to continue. Video chat?

☐ **I agree to this group covenant. Signed:** _____

(Keep this page as a reminder for yourself.)

How to Use this Material

This plan uses images, colors, and icons as cues and transitions for our visual culture:

 Pray. Open and close each lesson in prayer.

 Reflect. This is our built-in accountability, reinforcement, and reflection time.

 Media Placeholder. These help us capture the new topic with visual creativity.

Input Sections:

 Know Truth. Gain a basic but solid understanding of the topic.

 Process Truth. Digest and connect with the truth so we retain it.

Output Sections:

 Apply Truth. Be encouraged or equipped for action *as disciples*.

 Share Truth. Take the action past ourselves, and be encouraged *to disciple*.

The lead discipler of the group (the one bringing others along on this journey) needs to understand how vital the **Reflect, Apply Truth**, and **Share Truth** sections are. These are the parts that will separate this curriculum from other curricula and Bible studies that simply add knowledge. The lead discipler needs to reject any passive tendencies, and *set the example* of seeking to apply the material personally. It may be a new frontier for you as well. It may be messy. And that makes it a great growing experience!

Group Options

Here are a few suggested options for going through each lesson:

1) When you gather together, the group leader reads through the lesson out loud as the members follow along. Others in the group could read the Bible passages and special inset boxes to mix it up a bit. The benefits of this option are that the leader takes the initiative (but doesn't do *all* the reading), and there is no homework other than applying and sharing the lesson personally. It also provides opportunity to learn in community and have spontaneous questions or discussion about the material.

2) When you gather together, you read the material out loud, but the group members rotate reading through different sections. This mixes it up a little more than the first option. Again this has the benefit of no reading homework (just application and sharing homework). A potential drawback is that there may be someone who is not a strong out-loud reader, or who has a hard time comprehending content while they're concentrating on reading out loud.

3) Each member reads the lesson in advance and writes out their answers to the discussion questions. If they have questions about the text, they can write those in the margins. Benefits to this option are that the group could spend more time discussing the questions (and life), and it could be better for people who think they'd be distracted following along with out loud reading. Drawbacks are that you don't have the immediate opportunity for spontaneous questions or discussion about the text, and that people might not always do the reading homework. 😬

Each group should figure out which option or combination of options suits them. For example, if you start with the first option, as the members get used the material and begin growing, you could switch to the second option.

Part I: FOUNDATIONS

Since our foundation is what everything else is built on,
lessons from Part I will build our core framework for growth as disciples who disciple.

1. Telescope & Microscope [The Bible]

Pray

Open in prayer. Thank God for His salvation, His Word, and this time together. Ask God for His blessing and His insight as we discuss this topic.

Reflect

If your group size is bigger than two, make sure everyone knows one another. **Start with names and basic info if necessary.**

Since this is our first lesson, we don't have any material to reflect on yet. So let's share about our spiritual starting points.

What is your 90-second spiritual story?
If you've not put that into words before, here are some questions to get started:

    What were you like before Jesus?
    How did you come to learn about the Gospel?
    How/when/where did you respond to the Gospel?
    What is different about your life since accepting Christ?

    Or, if you're not quite sure you're there yet, share where you are at.

Have you ever been in a life group or other small group before?

Do you feel like you've been intentionally *discipled* before?

Media Placeholder: Telescope & Microscope

Telescopes and microscopes have been around for more than 4 centuries. They reveal truths about things that are beyond our natural scope of observation. Today, we have apps on our phones that can reveal the constellations even on a cloudy morning — and even beneath the horizon! We *can* and *do* observe the universe around us — it's just that we have a limited perspective without tools like these.

There are certain things we can observe about God just by beholding His handiwork.

> **Ps 19.1-4a (NIV)**
> *The heavens declare the glory of God;*
>   *the skies proclaim the work of his hands.*
> *2 Day after day they pour forth speech;*
>   *night after night they reveal knowledge.*
> *3 They have no speech, they use no words;*
>   *no sound is heard from them.*
> *4 Yet their voice goes out into all the earth,*
>   *their words to the ends of the world…*

The creation tells us *some* things about the Creator. Clues. For example, from simply observing creation, we might discern that the Creator is exceedingly powerful, intelligent, and creative… But that's about the extent of the picture we'll get of Him based on that natural observation. We need a *tool* to gain perspective of *Who God is* on a personal level, and *what His will is*.

The Bible is that tool. God has revealed Himself to today's generation through His written Word. The Bible reveals broad, sweeping truths like a telescope. And it reveals the intricate truths of our hearts like a microscope.

Many of us have looked through a telescope or microscope a handful of times. But you can bet an astronomer or microbiologist uses them quite frequently. Likewise, the Bible is a tool that Christians should *rely on*, not just occasionally peek into.

[The Bible]

Know Truth

Everything we need to know about *following God* is based on *knowing Him* and *knowing His will*. And since His Word is the tool that reveals that to us, the Bible will be the foundation that we build everything else on. So we need to make sure our foundation is solid and trustworthy!

Did you know?

All modern Bible translations are translated from the original Hebrew, Aramaic (in a small portion of the Old Testament), and Greek texts. They are not rewrites of other English translations. They are different attempts to put the original text into language we can best understand today.

So which translation should I use?

Probably not the King James Version. The KJV was "authorized" by King James of England in the 17th century. Four centuries ago, they used different pronouns, verb conjugations, etc, than we use today. So it's not really the language we speak.

Any modern translation should do, but if you have a choice, the ESV, NIV, and HCSB are especially good options that have a good balance of precision of words versus being easy to follow (in that order for the three). I use all three, but tend to land on ESV most. The HCSB is unique in that it uses American measuring units and capitalizes the pronouns for God. It also uses God's proper name, "Yahweh," when it is especially meaningful, whereas other translations use the traditional translation, "the LORD" (notice the "small caps" font case) where the Hebrew name *YHWH* is found.

The NASB is toward the end of the spectrum for word-for-word accuracy, but it's kind of on the wordy side. (Followed by the NKJV.[1]) The NLT is on the easy-to-follow side, but sometimes oversimplifies specifics. *The Message*[2] is at the extreme end of easy-to-follow, to the point of being more of a paraphrase, rather than an actual translation of the Bible.

Scripture: Take turns looking up the following Bible passages and reading them out loud. If anyone in the group is unfamiliar with how to navigate the Bible, or doesn't have one, take the time *now* to show them (*discipleship!*), and/or set them up with a Bible app on their smartphone. The "Bible" app by LifeChurch/YouVersion and the "Blue Letter Bible" are both good free apps.

Some people say the Bible was made up by people, or that what Christians say about the Bible wasn't even its original intent. With this in mind, **what do you observe about the origin and intentions of the Bible from these passages?**

Read Lk 1.1-4; Jn 19.35 & 21.24; 1Th 2.13; 2Pet 1.16,20-21.

Did you know?

The *Qur'an* and the *Book of Mormon* also claim to be the inspired word of God. Is there any *external* evidence (logical, bibliographical, archeological, etc) supporting the Bible, that sets it apart from other "sacred" books?

Yes, tons!

There's a whole field of study devoted to this, called Christian *apologetics*. For those who need the evidence, or are intrigued, here are some of the best resources: Look up books or videos by Josh McDowell, Lee Strobel, C.S. Lewis, or Nabeel Qureshi that deal with this subject. All 4 of these authors set out to disprove Christianity by uncovering the real evidence, but ended up becoming Christians themselves! Qureshi even came from a very strong Islamic background!

"After personally trying to shatter the historicity and validity of the Scriptures, I have been forced to conclude that they are historically trustworthy."[3]

— **Josh McDowell**

The following passages reveal 4 purposes of God's Word.

Read 2Tim 3.15-17; Jn 17.17; Mt 4.4.

Identify which verse each purpose was drawn from:

1) Providing us wisdom for salvation (_____)

2) Nourishing us (_____)

3) Sanctifying us (_____)

4) Equipping us for good works (_____)

Glossary: *Sanctify*

Sanctify means to make more holy or good. We are not 100% sanctified when we accept Jesus. In that moment, we are 100% *justified* —cleared of the charges against us— but only *beginning* to be sanctified. Sanctification is a life-long process as a disciple. It involves becoming more and more lined up with God's will.

 **Process Truth**

Discuss the following questions.

What experiences do you have with any of these purposes of God's Word? Which purpose would you like to experience more of?

Before looking into this material, did you have doubts or questions about whether the Bible is God's written Word? (If there's still any lingering doubt, be sure to study those apologetics resources until you've satisfied that doubt.)

Besides the Bible, there are *other* sources of influence that affect our beliefs and actions. Those other sources include things like culture, church doctrines, feelings, friends, Christian books, and parents. **Which of these have you had the hardest time *not* putting in front of the Bible, in shaping how you think and live? Why?**

Apply Truth

Throughout this discipleship guide, the *Apply Truth* section will feature specific ideas to put the lesson into practice. This first Apply Truth section focuses extra on equipping and preparing us *to* apply God's Word.

Read Matt 7.24-27; James 1.22-25.

God's Word is meant to be applied.
What insights do you gain about this from these two illustrations?

Read 2Tim 2.15.

Have you ever felt awkward or embarrassed about your lack of skill or knowledge about God's Word? Explain. Has that thought ever held you back from something?

If you *have* ever felt lacking in your Bible skills, did you take any action toward changing that?

Equipping Time.
In order to "correctly handle the Word of Truth," we'll need to become skilled in
    Understanding it,
    Getting it in us, and
    Taking action with what we learn.

Understanding the Bible

We've already started with the ideas that the Bible was inspired directly by God, and is His tool for us to know *Who He is* and *what His will is*. So here are a few basic helps for getting started with understanding God's Word the way He intends.

First, *don't complicate it.* God created the universe, the Bible, language, and you. Trust that He is able to use language to communicate His message to you in a way you can understand.
    The best understanding is the *most straightforward* understanding. That doesn't mean that every concept taught in the Bible is a simple idea, or easy to digest — just that we should approach each concept in the most straightforward way. For example, in **John 10.7&9**, when Jesus said, "I am the door," the straightforward understanding would be that He's using a *metaphor*, and didn't at that moment literally turn into wood! 😌 Likewise, if a passage was written as history, take it as history.

Second, *check the context.* Context also clarifies our understanding.
What is the context of this particular passage?
Who is it talking to?
Does God say anything else about the same topic in other passages?

Third, how should we approach the *Old Testament*?
We need to understand that the Old Testament contained *God's Law for the Jews*. So the big question is, do *Christians* need to obey the Old Testament? The Old Testament forbade things like tattoos, cotton-polyester shirts, and bacon.
    When Jesus ushered in the New Covenant, and non-Jewish people first started getting saved, the church leaders had a meeting to discuss this very question. And their conclusion was no, Christians do *not* need to keep the Law of Moses! You can read about that in Acts 15.
    But that does *not* mean the Old Testament should be ignored! The Old Testament gives us a deeper understanding of the *history* of our faith and the *character* of God, and is full of both positive and negative *examples* that we can learn from. It, also, should be understood straightforwardly. (Creation, Noah, Jonah, Song of Solomon? Yes! go with the most straightforward understanding of what was written.)

But as far as *obeying* God's Law, the *New Testament* contains *God's Law for Christians*. Many of God's Old Testament Laws were *repeated* in the New Testament, making them apply to us. Love God. Love your neighbor. Honor your parents. Don't steal. Don't follow idols. Etc. But if an Old Testament law was not re-commanded in the New Testament, that's one you should understand as applying specifically to Jews who lived before Christianity began. Freeing, isn't it? Bring on the bacon!

Matt 5.17 (ESV) *Do not think that I have come to abolish the Law or the Prophets; I have not come to abolish them but to fulfill them.*

Again, this was a stepping stone for application. We need to know how to approach God's Word with understanding before we can apply it.

Getting God's Word in us

Let's cut to the chase. I'm not going to truly know what the Bible says until I read it myself!

Have you read the *entire* Bible?

Does someone really *know* the Bible after reading through it once?

Do you have a plan in place already to get God's Word in you, or get His Word in you this *next* time?

If so, What is that plan?

How are you currently doing with it?

Taking Action

Our main application step for this first lesson is to *make sure we have a plan* to get God's Word in us, and to *set up accountability* with one another to encourage follow through.

If anyone in the group does not have a plan (or they've gotten bogged down in trying to just read straight through), take time *now*, in your group, to figure out your plans. Some hardcopy study Bibles have reading plans in the front or back. The "Blue Letter Bible" app has a handful of plans. The "Bible" app has *many* reading plans to choose from.

Suggestions

If you're brand new to the Bible, start with a reading plan that simply focuses on the New Testament. Straight through isn't a bad idea for the New Testament.

But if you have at least a *little* bit of Bible knowledge, start with a plan that goes through the entire Bible, but includes a New Testament reading each day. The LifeJournal plan[4] developed by Wayne Cordeiro, (available on the Bible app) goes through the Old Testament once, and New Testament twice, over the course of a year. It usually includes about 3 Old Testament chapters and 1 New Testament chapter each day.

If you prefer a paper Bible, a pretty simple plan is to get two bookmarks. Put one in Genesis and one in Matthew. Read about 3 Old Testament chapters, then switch over to a New Testament chapter. Do that each day, and you'd be through the whole Bible in a year. (You can always restart the New Testament if you get through that first.)

But there's nothing sacred about doing it in 1 year. Choose a two-year plan if you prefer. Or read one chapter of Old Testament and New Testament each day. Or slam through it in 90 days for a big picture overview (about 12 chapters per day). It's up to you.

The point is to have a plan because you want to get God's Word in you, so you can know Him and His will, and begin to disciple others along the way!

If you don't already have a plan, **take time *now* to choose your plan.**
Don't spend forever on your decision — it's only a starting point.
When you finish this plan, you can repeat it if you really liked it, or choose a different one.

 ## Share Truth

The first way to take this past yourself is to share your Bible plan with your discipleship group and ask them to keep you accountable with it. Why? to be legalistic? No! to get more of God's Word in you, so you can know Him and His will, and begin to disciple others along the way!

What level of accountability will that take? Will you need reminders before next week? If so, how often? Who will provide those to whom?

How will you bring today's lesson to someone *outside* this group?
You might check certain boxes as goals, or add your own.

☐ **Share about a new confidence in approaching God's Word.**

☐ **Show someone how to use a Bible app.**

☐ **Show someone how to find a reading plan on a Bible app.**

☐ **Make a Bible reading plan printout available to someone.**

☐ **Give a physical Bible to someone.**

☐ **Post about what God's showing you, or about what you're starting.**

☐ **Talk with someone in person about it.**

☐ **Post a "verse image" from a passage that really struck you today.**

☐ **Grab a friend and show them (or figure out together) how to look up keywords in a Bible concordance, app, or website. How do you search for multiple words, or exclude certain words to thin the results?**

Is God inspiring you with any *different ideas* for bringing this to the next person?

☐

☐

Share with your group how you're going to bring this past your group.

Matt 28.18-20 (ESV) *And Jesus came and said to them, "All authority in heaven and on earth has been given to me. ¹⁹ Go therefore and make disciples of all nations, baptizing them in the name of the Father and of the Son and of the Holy Spirit, ²⁰ teaching them to observe all that I have commanded you. And behold, I am with you always, to the end of the age."*

Making disciples involves teaching obedience of all Jesus commanded.
That starts with getting His Word in me — so I can know Who He is and what His will is.

Pray

1 *New King James Version®*. Copyright © 1982 by Thomas Nelson.
2 *The Message*. Copyright © 1993, 1994, 1995, 1996, 2000, 2001, 2002 by NavPress Publishing Group.
3 Josh McDowell, *More than a Carpenter* (USA; Living Books, 1977) 55.
4 Wayne Cordeiro, *LifeJournal* (© Life Resources).

2. Life Preserver Ring [The Gospel]

Pray

Reflect

Last week we talked about wanting to get God's Word in us, so we can know Him and His will, and begin to disciple others along the way.

How have you done with getting God's Word in you over last 7 days?
(Don't be vague; this is your team.)

What was most memorable or impactful from this past week's reading?

In what way(s) did you bring last week's lesson to someone outside our group?

Media Placeholder: Life Preserver Ring

The life preserver ring is one of our most basic pictures of life-saving. It represents life and death. It's clear. It's simple.

Upon seeing the need, none of us would hesitate to use it. We wouldn't make excuses. We wouldn't worry about whether we were *qualified* to use it, or whether the person drowning might *reject* our help. Neither would we *ignore* the need. We'd see a person drowning, we'd spot the life preserver, and we'd make every effort to get that life-saving device to them.

There is clear urgency when it comes to saving someone's physical life — which is only temporary. So why is there not *much more urgency* about saving someone's *soul* — which is eternal?

The Gospel is *the* life-saving device God has provided for rescuing souls. The stakes are *literally* heaven or hell forever. Yet most Christians only grasp enough of the Gospel to respond to it themselves… but not enough to articulate it to someone else. Some Christians confuse "having a spiritual conversation" with "sharing the Gospel." The first can open the door for the second, but they are *not* the same. The Gospel is something *very specific*, not just a vague interest or belief or "like" in Jesus or church.

The Gospel is our <u>only</u> spiritual life-saving device. Yet it's not as simple to use as, "see the lifesaver ring, throw it." We need to *own* the *what*, *why*, and *how* of the Gospel — enough to communicate it clearly. And when we do that, it both motivates and prepares us to save lives.

Gen 45.7 (NIV) *But God sent me ahead of you to preserve for you a remnant on earth and to save your lives by a great deliverance.*

God sent Jacob's son Joseph ahead of his family to preserve their physical lives from famine, like a life preserver that is strategically placed —in advance— to save someone's life.

And God is sending *you*, right now, ahead of a family member, a friend, or someone you don't even know yet — to preserve their spiritual life for *eternity*. This lesson is your equipping opportunity. First, make sure you've understood and responded on the *receiving* end. But whether this lesson is new material or review for you, make sure you open your eyes and ears to the *sharing* side of the Gospel as well.

14

[The Gospel]

Know Truth

We're going to go through the Gospel visually, using a unique version of the bridge diagram.[1] We'll lay it out by following some step-by-step instructions — for you to be able to share it with someone else. Of course there are many different styles and many different levels of detail you could use to share the Gospel. But for *this* equipping time, we're going to go through it *thoroughly* and step by step, so we can develop a solid understanding. After going through these instructions once or twice, you'll probably be able to share it with someone by simply looking at the finished product and recreating it on a blank sheet of paper. All you'll need to remember is the basic flow.

There's a template page found at the end of this lesson. You could flip back and forth to that as you fill it out. Or you could print off a copy at http://svsu.hhcf.org/gospel-template/. (The leader could print these off in advance.) Here are the basic instructions for using this Gospel guide:

- *Instructions* are in *italic square brackets []*.

- Regular text is something you might say out loud while going through this with someone.

- **Key statements** and ideas are in **bold**.

- Things to **be sure to write** are in **"bold quotation marks."**

- Each of the following shaded boxes in this section corresponds to the light-gray box on the template with the matching number. Use these to figure out your spatial arrangement the first time, since your page will be full.

- When going through this with someone who needs to hear the Gospel, you can draw this out for them, then give them the paper at the end. Or, you could give them a sheet to fill out themselves as you go through it together.

If you've been through this material before and your diagram is already filled in (or you're using an electronic version of this book), print off a new copy or recreate the drawing starting with a blank sheet of paper and two circles.

Again, this is a *thorough* version of the Gospel. But there may be occasions when you don't have time to go through the full version with someone. Or the person you're talking to may be wired in a way that they'd be satisfied with the basics. For a *super-simple version,* the highlighted portions cover the most basic key ideas of the Gospel. That abbreviated version is short enough and simple enough to write out on the back of a business card or to enter as a simple note in your phone. That way you can be ready to share the basics any time and place! Yet this detailed version we're about to cover will equip and train you to deeply understand the Gospel well enough to elaborate on the simple version and answer some basic questions.

The Gospel (Good News) of Jesus Christ.

As we go through this, if you have any questions, please interrupt me to ask.

First we're going to set up our visual...

[1] Read "Mt 12.26&28." *[Write that scripture reference in box "1" directly under the title.]*

Jesus names two spiritual kingdoms in these verses. What are they?

[2] *[Put labels <u>above</u> the two circles on your diagram. The **"kingdom of Satan"** on the left,*

[3] *and the **"Kingdom of God"** on the right.]*

Without exception, every person on earth belongs to one of these two spiritual kingdoms. Not that many people would choose to be part of Satan's kingdom, it's just that if someone does *not* belong to God's kingdom, the other one is the only other option — whether they realize this or not.

[Put alternative labels and descriptions <u>inside</u> the circles.]

[4] The kingdom of Satan is also known as the "World"...

[5] and includes "anyone who's guilty of sin."
The citizens of this kingdom range from the truly evil person to the really nice person.

[6] The Kingdom of God is also known as the "Church."

[7] and includes "anyone who is innocent (like a baby or child)**,
perfect** (which only describes Jesus)**,
or freed from their guilt."**
The citizens of God's Kingdom range from 'baby' to mature in faith.

Now we're going to look at the Why, the What, and the How of the Gospel.

THE WHY:
**It starts with God's moral character that He's revealed through His Word.
There are 2 *equal* sides to God's nature.**

[8] "His nature:" *[Write that in the top right margin near "Kingdom of God."]*
[For each reference, look it up first, then write it with its summary.]
"1Jn 4.8 — God is Love." *[Write this under "His nature."]*
*[Want to dig deeper or need clarification?
See these additional passages: Rom 8.38-39; Eph 3.16-19; 1Jn 3.1]*

God is the author of love and the epitome of perfect, selfless, unconditional love. (NOT to be confused with "niceness.") Qualities like His *grace* and *kindness* are part of His *loving* nature.

"Rev 16.5 — God is Holy." *[Write this just below "God is Love."]*
[Lk 1.49; Rev 15.4; 2Th 1.5-6]

He is morally perfect, and a perfectly just and righteous Judge. Qualities like His *justice* and His *fierce anger against sin* are part of His *holy* nature.

Since we're comparing kingdoms, let's take a brief look at the other kingdom ruler.
[In the left margin, near "Kingdom of Satan"…]

[9] "his nature:"
"Rev 12.9 — Satan is a deceiver."

Now here's where *we* come into play…
[In the left margin near the bottom left of the World circle…]

[10] "Our Nature:"
"Rom 3.23 — All of us have sinned."
[Rom 3.10-12; James 2.10; James 4.17]

No surprises here… Every one of us has done something we knew was wrong, or failed to do something we knew was right.

So how does God's nature respond to our nature?

[11] "God's holiness *must punish* sin." *[under the World circle]*
"Rom 2.5 — wrath"
"Rom 6.23a — wage" ('a' refers to the first half of the verse)
"Rev 20.10,14-15 — hell"

[Draw an arrow from the left circle to the word "hell."]
This is the destination of anyone found in this kingdom at the end of their life.
[Rom 14.12; 2Th 1.6-9]

It would be *against God's nature* to let *any* sin go unpunished. That punishment for sin is eternity in hell — a living death, away from God's presence forever. That is what we *earn* (the "wage") for our sinful actions; it's what we *deserve* before a holy God.

This is our predicament. **This is the *bad news* that leads into the *Good News*!**

[On the right side, just under the church's circle...]
But remember God's other side...

[12] "God's love *compels Him to forgive* and restore us."
   "Rom 5.6-8 — love"
   "Rom 6.23 — gift" (full verse)
   "Rev 21.1-6 — heaven"
   [Draw an arrow from the right circle to the word "heaven."]

He created us for a relationship with Him, so His love drives Him to make a way for us to be with Him forever.

That was all the Why; now let's look at
THE WHAT:

[Middle of the page, just under everything else...]
So this would seem to put the two sides of God's nature at odds...
But in response to our sin,

[13] "God did the only thing that would satisfy both sides of His nature:
   He became our substitute! — 1Pet 3.18; Rom 3.22-26"
      [Col 2.13-14; Heb 7.24-27; Heb 9.27-28; 2Tim 1.9-10; 1Jn 2.2]

God the Son entered humanity (as Jesus Christ),
   lived a perfect sinless life (so He didn't owe the punishment Himself).
Then He *willingly took our punishment* (as our substitute).

His physical death was *in place of* our spiritual death of hell.
Then He conquered death forever by rising from the grave!

Since God is eternal and infinite,
   Jesus' one sacrifice was sufficient to cover any number of people
   — but only those who accept His offer!

[Continuing down]

[14] "Jesus' offer is free and unearnable — Eph 2.8-9"
      [Rom 4.4-5; Titus 3.4-7]

Community service can never undo a death sentence. Even if our good works outweigh our bad 100 to 1, our sin still deserves the punishment of hell. So we *cannot ever earn* God's forgiveness. But He offers that forgiveness *freely* as a *gift*, based on His love and His sacrifice. This is *grace*.

Here's an illustration to drive home the relationship between justice, mercy, and grace.[2]
Let's say you were driving 57mph in a 45mph zone and get pulled over.
If the officer writes you up a ticket for the exact amount you were speeding (12 over), that is justice.

[15] "Justice – deserved punishment"

If the officer lets you off with a warning, that is mercy.
"Mercy – exemption from punishment"
(But it wasn't *justice*.)

If the officer writes you up for the full amount,
then hands you cash out of his own wallet to pay for the ticket, that is grace.
"Grace – undeserved gift"
(*Justice* was also served since the crime was paid for.
And it was also *mercy* because you didn't pay the penalty yourself.)

[Continuing…]

[16] "Count the cost — Lk 14.28-33; Mt 13.18,20-23"
[Mt 7.21-23; 1Cor 6.19-20; 1Pet 4.12-13]
Jesus' offer is completely and totally *free* in the sense that we <u>cannot earn it</u> — yet it comes with *expectation*. We have to agree to the terms and conditions, so to speak. It's not about starting; it's about following through — in the blessings and the trials.
"Accepting His offer means accepting His authority over your life."

We can live for ourselves — and pay the price for our sin ourselves. Or we can let God purchase our life-debt with the blood of Jesus — and we become His disciples.

[17] "Forgiven instantly; more holy over time.
    Rom 4.23-5.2 — Justification; Php 1.6 — Sanctification"
    [Heb 7.24-25; 1Thes 4.1-7; 1Cor 6.9-11]

As we mentioned in the first lesson, this is the difference between the big churchy words *justification* and *sanctification*. When we become Christians, we instantly go from being 0% forgiven to 100% forgiven. This is *justification* — we are completely cleared before the Judge. The crime has been paid for in full. Jesus' sacrifice covers all our sins (including future mess-ups).
    Then once we are saved from God's punishment, *sanctification* is the process of us becoming more and more holy (good) over time. It happens as we listen to God's Word and the Holy Spirit and seek to become more like Jesus.

There is no expectation to be instantly perfect or have it all together the moment you commit to Jesus — just the expectation to allow God to keep growing your faith and obedience over time!

So when we broke God's law, we excluded ourselves from His Kingdom.
But He has provided *one way* to get *out of* the kingdom of Satan,
      and *into* the Kingdom of God.

[18] "Jn 14.6"
    *[Draw the outline of a **cross** to bridge the gap between the two circles (around box 20.)]*
       [Acts 4.10-12]

*[Put an **arrow** arching over the cross from left to right]*
Because of our sin and God's holiness,

[19] "Jesus is the *only way*" to heaven.
    [Write this over the arc of the arrow.]

Every other religion attempts to *earn* a better afterlife (or present life) through *works* — being good, following the rules, etc. But biblical Christianity is the *only faith* where the punishment for sin is *completely paid for* by God.
      In His holiness, God *did not have to* provide a way for us to escape His wrath against sin. But thanks be to Jesus that in His love, He offers a way!

THE HOW.
How do we accept God's free offer?

Even though Jesus died for the sins of *potentially* everybody,
    it's obvious that not everyone is a Christian.
What makes the distinction? How and when is Jesus' offer applied to our individual account?

[20] The Bible teaches a simple 4-part response to accept Jesus' offer.
    *[Write the word **"Respond"** across the crossbar of the cross.]*

The 4 parts work together. None of them are attempts to earn our salvation; they are only responses to God's gracious offer. And when we follow all 4, we can have *full assurance* of God's forgiveness, adoption into His family, and eternity in heaven.

[21] "Rom 10.9-10 & Acts 2.37-38"
    [Write these under "Respond," across the bottom of the cross.]

    "•Believe in Jesus."
        [Jn 3.16; Acts 10.43; Mk 16.16; 1Tim 1.16; James 2.19]
    Believe that He died for your sins, then conquered death by rising from the grave.
    Belief is the *foundation* and *prerequisite*— all the other parts of our response hinge on this one!

But He asks for *more than* belief.

"·Repent of sin."
    [Acts 3.19; Rom 6.1-2; Mk 1.15]
This means we regret our wrongs and turn toward pursuing God now instead of pursuing sin in our life.

"·Proclaim Jesus as Lord."
    [Mt 10.32; 1Jn 4.15]
This is a declaration and commitment that I am no longer the king of my life — Jesus is.

"·Be Baptized" (Immersed in water as your own decision).
    [Rom 6.3-4; 1Pet 3.18-21; Mk 16.16; Jn 3.3-5; Acts 22.16]
Baptism is the culmination of the responses. It's a powerful physical demonstration of pledging yourself to Jesus. It illustrates the death to your old life, resurrection to your new life in Christ, and your acceptance of His freely offered grace and Lordship.

What's next? After someone responds to become a follower of Jesus, you would invite them into a **discipleship group** like this one! Imagine if every new follower of Jesus began their journey by learning to become a disciple who disciples!

 Process Truth

In going through these details about the Gospel, what was most helpful? Deeper understanding? Reinforcement? Drawing it out on paper?

Did you pick up on anything that you hadn't before?

If you've been committed to follow Jesus for some time, but missed any of the biblical response pieces, there's no need to panic. If you already consider Jesus your Lord, simply bring that attitude to fruition by following through, and celebrate! We'll ask specifically about that in **Apply Truth** section.

(Would you like to learn more about Christian baptism? See **Appendix B**. It's a resource that could be studied individually or as a group together.)

Remember, this is the *Gospel*. It was *not* all the situations, conversations, or relationships that may *lead into* the Gospel. Those will vary a lot from person to person. But let's say you've been talking with someone, and you sense they may be at a point of being *ready to hear* the Gospel. (Let's also assume you can schedule a one-on-one and have access to a resource like this.)

Where is your confidence level in your ability to tell someone the why, what, and how of becoming a Christian?

Is that level different from before we went through this?

 Apply Truth

Have you *personally* applied the truth of the Gospel by responding in all 4 ways the Bible describes?

If any piece was missing, is there anything that would hold you back from applying that now?

Did you know?

The New Testament never instructs us to respond to God's offer by "asking Jesus into our heart" or even by praying a sinner's prayer. Neither does it tell us to respond by raising our hand while everyone else's eyes are closed.

When we oversimplify the Gospel (whether in the offer or in the response) we miss an opportunity to pass along clarity and assurance. We miss the opportunity to start them on a journey of looking to God's Word for the answers and trusting those answers.

However, when we share the *biblical why, what,* and *how* of the Gospel with someone, they'll know with *certainty* whether or not they're a Christian. There won't be any lingering doubts about whether they're *really* in, or why another religion isn't just as valid. That's because they'll see the big picture and know that they've responded to accept God's free offer in the way He invites us to through His Word.

Have you *clearly* shared the Gospel with someone before?
(We're not just talking about having a spiritual conversation.)

If so, did they *clearly* respond in the 4 ways God's Word teaches?

Again, a simple way you could always be *prepared* to share the Gospel would be to copy the highlighted key ideas onto a small reminder card that you could keep in your wallet, purse, backpack, or vehicle. Or enter them as a note on your phone!

Share Truth

Rom 10.13-15 (NIV) *for, "Everyone who calls on the name of the Lord will be saved."* [14] *How, then, can they call on the one they have not believed in? And how can they believe in the one of whom they have not heard? And how can they hear without someone preaching to them?* [15] *And how can anyone preach unless they are sent? As it is written: "How beautiful are the feet of those who bring good news!"*

Eph 6.14-15 (HCSBS) *Stand, therefore, with truth like a belt around your waist, righteousness like armor on your chest,* [15] *and your feet sandaled with readiness for the gospel of peace.*

God connects the Gospel with our feet *twice* in the New Testament. It's something we are meant to *bring to* others. And of course we need to *use words* to communicate that Good News as well. (That's why our "Share Truth" icon represents both these ideas! 😉)

***Who* do you think God wants you to share the Good News with? (specifically)**

When you talk with someone who you never talked with about spiritual things before, how can you find out where they're at with Jesus?
        What specific questions might you ask them to find out?
(*Hint:* Asking about a church background might be a good *starting point*, but that doesn't actually tell us if they've *heard or responded* to the Gospel…)

Sharing our **90-second spiritual story** (from Lesson 1's **Reflect** section) could help open a door for someone to want to hear more about knowing Jesus. As we attempt to share the Gospel with others, it's helpful to remember it's *all about relationships!* God wants a relationship with them, and building actual friendships is always the best approach to spreading the Gospel. It's not healthy (or generally effective) to view people as "projects" to be saved.
        You may need to lay some additional groundwork before you perceive someone is ready to hear the Gospel. It often doesn't happen all in one sitting (but it might).

What steps are you going to take this week to start working toward a Gospel opportunity with the person(s) God brought to your mind?

☐

☐

Pray

Pray together for opportunities.

---

1 Thank you Bob Russell for this idea of the "two kingdoms" bridge diagram.
2 Thank you Bob Russell for this idea of the speeding ticket illustration.

The Gospel: The Good News of Jesus

The Gospel: The Good News of Jesus

3. Empty Bench [Pursuing Vital Relationships]

Pray

Reflect

How have you done over that last 7 days with getting God's Word in you? (Again, don't be vague; this is your team.)

What was most memorable or impactful from your time in God's Word this week?

Last time we were equipped with the big picture Gospel.
If you had realized any of the response pieces were missing from your own response, did you take any steps toward that this week?

Did you start pursuing a God-opportunity with the person He brought to your mind last week? Where are you at with that?

In what others way(s) did you bring last week's lesson to someone outside our group?

Media Placeholder: Empty Bench

Think about this empty bench. It's not a bench overlooking a beautiful landscape; in fact the location doesn't really matter. It's just a bench. But it's in front of you, and no one's on it.

If this bench were symbolic of *relationships* in your life (not just a quiet place to sit), it might represent either end of a spectrum. It may be a reminder of *loneliness*, because no one's there — as usual. ☹

Or, at the other end of the spectrum, you may see it as *opportunity* — this is a place you could sit down with someone and invest in a relationship! 😃

Most of us probably fall somewhere in the middle — maybe a little closer to one end or the other. But it raises the question: Am I *pursuing* healthy relationships?

In **Genesis 2.18**, God said that it's not good for us humans to be alone. God designed you and I in *His* image. And that image includes a built-in need for *community*. Even before God created any other beings —whether human or angelic— *He* was never alone. As the Trinity, God the Father, God the Son, and God the Holy Spirit lived in perfect fellowship before time began. And He hard-wired us for that too!

But we live in a broken world. We've witnessed broken relationships. We've been hurt *personally*, and that makes it hard to trust. We hate loneliness. Yet our fear of rejection tempts many of us to see loneliness (or *surfaceness*) as the "safe" alternative.

Or perhaps we don't *fear* relationships; we're just too *distracted* by personal entertainment, success, _____ — so that we don't give community the time it needs. But whether fears or distractions keep us from investing deeply in relationships, that ultimately results in lose-lose situations for both ourselves and the people around us. (Despite what we may tell ourselves.)

Prov 18.1 (ESV) *Whoever isolates himself seeks his own desire;*
he breaks out against all sound judgment.

Did it ever occur to you that *not* investing in relationships was a sign of *selfishness*? The Proverb goes on to say any excuses we might make about it go against wisdom.

No matter what has held us back from *deeper* fellowship (whatever our starting level), it's time to start building that community. In this lesson, we'll look at 3 vital relationships God designed His followers to pursue. And as God gives us little reminders of those relationships each day, picture that empty bench as being ready and waiting to be filled.

[Pursuing Vital Relationships]

Know Truth

God designed His disciples to pursue 3 types of vital relationships, and those follow a logical order. First is our relationship with God. Second is our relationship with a community of Christians. Third is our relationship with seekers and non-believers (anyone who has not clearly responded to God's offer). We'll take a look at these in order.

Why is that?
Why wasn't a romantic relationship included in the top 3?
Some people have the gift of singleness, such as the Apostle Paul (**1Cor 7.7**). Even though most of us *deeply desire* a romantic relationship, it is *not vital* for being a growing disciple. And for those who are *in* a romantic relationship, as **2Cor 6.14** instructs, that relationship should be *part of* the Christian community we are pursuing. But all of us can use *more* Christian community than just one person.

Pursuing a relationship with God

Accepting the Gospel means we *have* a relationship with God, but that says nothing about the *state* of that relationship. The <u>parents</u> of a runaway still *technically* have a relationship with their child, but it is not a *good* relationship.

Or consider a <u>marriage</u> relationship. Would you say a married couple has a good relationship if they only ever see each other for a total of an hour or two per week? Even worse if that hour is all one way communication, right? Yet many Christians consider an hour or two in church or church activities every week sufficient for their relationship with God. For some people, it's even less than that because of their "busyness."

Yet when our relationship with God is not close, God's not the one at fault. The Bible uses these same illustrations as above, with God as our <u>Father</u>, and as the <u>Husband</u> of the church.

In **Lk 15.11-32**, Jesus tells the story of the "prodigal son." He likens God to the father who keeps an eager watch for his son's return — in order to show him love and grace. This was the same son who basically told him, "Drop dead and give me my inheritance now."

Hosea 3.1 likens God's pursuit of us to a husband who loves and pursues his wife even *while* she's pursuing adultery. God always desires a deeper and closer relationship with us — flaws and all! We never have to fear His rejection!

But if we're going to have a *good* relationship, we have to *pursue Him* as well!

Read Mt 22.36-38.

Jesus said that *the most important thing* we can do is to love God with our everything! That means being on the *pursuing* side, and not just the *receiving* side of the relationship. And just like any human relationship,

> **Our best relationship with God will involve communicating together, doing things together, and spending time together.**

As far as doing things together with God, it's okay to think outside the box. In his book, *Sacred Pathways*,[1] Gary Thomas wrote about 9 different ways people tend to connect with God. Andy Stanley's church once did a series on this book and came up with some creative drama skits to go along with it. (That series DVD, "You've Got Style," is available for purchase at store.northpoint.org. Focus on the Family has posted a free survey to help pinpoint your worship style. Here's an easy link to that: http://svsu.hhcf.org/discover/)

Think about the ways you've felt most connected with God — not necessarily in a church service. It may have been when you've walked through a forest, or when you've taken action with a cause God cares about, or when you've journaled. Seeking to implement more of your God-connection activities into your relationship with Him can be a great way to strengthen your personal closeness with Him!

Our relationship with God is *by far*, the *most important relationship* to invest our time and energy in as His followers!

Pursuing relationships in a Christian community

There is a growing sentiment of people today who think it's fine to be Christians apart from the Church. They say things like, "I like Jesus, but I don't like the church." But…
Trying to follow God *apart from* a community of believers is trying to live outside of God's plan for your life!

Remember how God said that it was not good for Adam to be alone? God designed us for a relationship with *Him*, but He also designed us to need *one another*.

Read Eph 2.19-22; Rom 12.4-5.

God wants us to see our fellow Christians as neighbors, family members, and even as essential as various parts of the human body!

Read Heb 10.24-25.

We need other Christians in our lives to love us, challenge us, and encourage us. (And vice versa!) As **Prov 18.1** pointed out in the intro to this lesson, to isolate ourselves from that is selfish. It also goes against wisdom, since building that community will result in mutual blessings.

Will it be messy? Will we encounter some hypocrites along the way? Of course! But without the love, challenge, and encouragement of a spiritual family, we'll never reach God's potential for us as disciples — simply because He designed us that way!

Just like with building our relationship with God,

Pursuing relationships with seekers and non-Christians

If you've ever been on an airplane, you may remember something from the flight attendant's announcement at the beginning of the flight. If the oxygen masks drop down at some point, you're instructed to put *your* mask on first, *then* assist other people. That's kind of the idea behind pursuing relationships with seekers and non-Christians. Our relationship with God and a community of Christians has more to do with our *health*. And when those are in place, they will *empower us* to help others and pursue our *mission* of reaching others.

That's why we put these relationships in this order of priority. If we get them out of order, or skip any of them, we're not going to be effective disciples.

For example, some Christians try to bypass Christian community because they are so focused on building relationships with the lost. But when this happens, it's often a predictable result: over time they will become less and less of an influence on their lost friends, and the lost friends will become more and more of an influence on the Christian. Their relationship with God will suffer, even if they seemed "on fire" for Him at the beginning.

Read 1Cor 15.33.

On the other hand, some Christians are so scared of (or snooty about) that bad influence, that they completely surround themselves with a Christian bubble, and end up not investing in *any* non-Christian relationships. But then if they have no relationships outside the church, how are they to fulfill their *mission* of making *new* disciples?

Read 1Cor 9.19-23.

The apostle Paul did his best to *relate* with non-Christians (build relationships) *so that* he could be a *witness* to them.

This third relationship will require the same relational ingredients in order to be most effective.

Building bridges with non-Christians will involve communicating together, doing things together, and spending time together.

But we need to keep that pursuit in our context of priority.

Gal 6.10 (NIV) *Therefore, as we have opportunity, let us do good to all people, <u>especially</u> to those who belong to the family of believers.*

Yes, God wants us to invest in non-Christians. But after our relationship with Him, our *next priority* is to take care of *family*. *Then* come the others (who are hopefully future family).

Process Truth

Have you previously thought of all 3 of these relationships as being "vital" to your Christian walk?

As you think about it now, are all three vital in the same way? Explain.

In what ways do you think you best connect with God?
How often do you incorporate that into your time with God?

Would you say the amount of time and energy you invest in these 3 relationships lines up with the order they should be prioritized in?

Which relationship is most lacking compared to where it should be?

Apply Truth

What do I see as my best opportunities for pursuing Christian community?
How can I improve the *depth* of my Christian community?

What are my best opportunities for pursuing friendships with seekers or non-Christians?

What adjustments need to be made to my schedule in order to pursue these relationship types in the proper order?
    What do I need to say *no* to in order to say *yes* to this? (*Accountability?*)

As a discipleship group, what are ways we could fellowship together beyond these discipleship meetings?

As an *assignment*, take the worship styles survey (45 questions) found at http://svsu.hhcf.org/discover/.

☐ **Record your results to share with us next week.**

Share Truth

If we apply the ideas of investing in Christian community and in the lost, we're automatically bringing it to the next person. That's kind of built into this topic.

Are there any specific people I feel I should start with?

As we work on the depth of our personal relationship with God, one way to bring that to the next person would be to…

☐ **share the link to the worship styles survey and post your results.**

What other ways could we bring this lesson to the next person?

☐

☐

 **Pray**

---

1 Gary Thomas, *Sacred Pathways: Discovering Your Soul's Path to God* (Grand Rapids, MI; Zondervan, 2000).

Part II: BEYOND THE PHYSICAL

2Cor 4.18 (NIV) *So we fix our eyes not on what is seen, but on what is unseen, since what is seen is temporary, but what is unseen is eternal.*

A disciple's power has much *more* to do with the unseen than the seen.
Spiritual interactions can propel us forward, or send us backward.
Part II equips us to better connect with God and engage the enemy.

4. Sync Cable [Prayer & Fasting]

Pray

Reflect

Last time we learned about pursuing 3 relationships vital to our discipleship. Those relationships were with God, with a community of believers, and with the lost. We saw how communicating together, doing things together, and spending time together were key ingredients for all 3 and that we should keep them prioritized.

Which of these key ingredients did you try to implement more this week?
With whom? How did it go?

Share your worship style results.

Did the survey provide any helpful insights about yourself
or about how others are wired differently from you?

Were you inspired to try anything new in your worship of God?

How have you done over that last 7 days with getting God's Word in you?
If anyone in the group has fallen behind from their goal, what will it take (from the rest of the group) to help get you on track until you've formed a *habit* of reading the Bible?
(Don't forget that the reason for making a habit is because of our desire to know God better by getting His Word in us.)

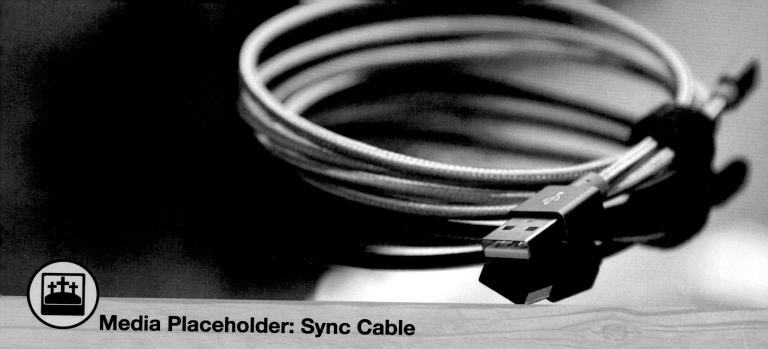

Media Placeholder: Sync Cable

Since the invention of the smart phone, many of us cannot imagine life without something similar to this. A sync cable charges our battery and synchronizes our data. Even if we sync our phone with an online cloud rather than a computer, much of that still happens when we're plugged in (or when our wireless charger is plugged in).

Wouldn't it be awesome to have a sync cable that plugs us straight into God?

1Tim 1.17 (ESV) *To the King of the ages, immortal, invisible, the only God, be honor and glory forever and ever. Amen.*

Even though God is very real, He's invisible. And as residents of the physical universe, we are easily distracted by the here and now. For that reason alone, developing a closer relationship with God is going to require *more intentionality* than our relationships with the people we can see and hear and touch. So we could really use some sort of *direct connection* with Him.

In Lesson 1, we learned about the importance of getting God's Word in us. That's like the download part — the primary way God gets His instructions into us. But we need more than a one-way sync. A good relationship requires two-way communication! That's where prayer comes in.

Prayer is our sync cable with God!

We've been praying to open and close our meetings. And I'm sure you thought of prayer when we talked about communicating together with God. But many Christians have a very limited experience and understanding of prayer. Is prayer merely a ritual we perform at Christian meetings, at meal time, and maybe when traveling or just before bed? Is it our last hope after we've tried everything else? Does it always sound exactly the same? Do we mainly see it as how we *get* things?

If you had a friend who only communicated with you the way many people communicate with God, how close of a friendship would that be? You probably wouldn't feel very in tune with that person, or empowered by them. That's because a friendship's not designed to run on such a small, imbalanced view of communication. And neither is our relationship with God.

What if you neglected to charge your phone? How long would it be able to do the things it's intended to do? Likewise, we can't expect to be very functional as disciples without having a full and regular sync with God. Combined with the Word, prayer can be that.

[Prayer]

 Know Truth

There are literally *hundreds* of Bible verses about prayer. So there are many, many ideas that we *could* unpack about it. But we're going to keep it simple by zeroing in on 2 main purposes of prayer, then sharing 3 power up tips. All the other purposes for prayer can tie into these 2 primary purposes. And they follow from our Media Placeholder illustration: synchronizing and charging.

A disciple prays in order to get in tune with God and to ask Him to demonstrate His power.

Praising God, thanking God, expressing love to God, confessing sin, asking for wisdom, or seeking attitude adjustments — all of those (plus similar prayers) help to *line us up* with Who God is. And it honors God when we do this.

Read Ps 139.23-24.

Many of the Psalms are prayers that reflect that desire to be in sync with God.

Praying for specific people to be saved, asking for opportunities, requesting deliverance, seeking justice, asking for healing, etc, are all invitations for God to *demonstrate His power* in our lives and the lives around us.

Read Eph 3.20-21.

So many prayer requests ask for such small or insignificant things that we wouldn't even recognize if God answered yes. For example, "Bless this food to our bodies," or "Be with us." Not that those are bad things to pray, but if those are the *extent* of our prayers, we're never going to see God move in power. He has the power to grant *immeasurably more* than we could ask or imagine. Doesn't that entice you to start imagining and asking for some pretty big things?

Are there *limits* to those requests?
Only in the sense that the power part is directly tied to the being in sync part.

The more our hearts and requests are in tune with God's heart, the more likely He'll answer yes.

Read James 4.3.

When we pray about something and God's answer is no, that *does not mean* He doesn't love us or doesn't have the power to change the situation! It simply means we weren't lined up with His will or the timing wasn't right. Sometimes He even denies an otherwise good request because we weren't ready for it, or because He knows that this other path will ultimately result in something *better*. For example, maybe denying one person's physical healing will ultimately lead to another person's salvation. Maybe denying this job will result in a push toward personal maturity or a deeper reliance on God.

It's not our job to guess what His answer will be before we decide to ask. There's no way we could imagine all the factors God sees.

Our job is simply to seek to get in tune with Him and ask Him to demonstrate His power.

Read Php 4.6.

Thanking God helps remind us of Who He is — that aligning part. Then we simply put the requests in front of Him. No need to qualify the requests or make any guess about God's answer or timing. We simply give Him our requests and trust Him to answer them in the best way.

Again there is so much to learn and apply about prayer that it will be a lifelong process. We're just looking to start heading in the right direction as disciples.

3 Power Ups for Prayer.

There are 3 secret ingredients that can improve both the *in-tune* and the *power* parts to our prayers. They're actually not "secret" at all — nor are they "cheat" codes — it's just that most Christians fail to employ these aids to their prayer lives in any sort of regular way.

1) Fasting.

Read Ezra 8.23; Acts 13.2-3.

Fasting is when we give up something from our lives (usually food) <u>for the purpose of</u> spending more time with God in prayer. Christian fasting is not just giving up something for the sake of giving up something! It's not just failing to eat. It's going without, <u>so that</u> we can better tune in and be more receptive to God's power at work in us.

In **Jn 6.35**, Jesus called Himself the "Bread of Life." In **Mt 4.4**, He said that "man does not live on bread alone, but by every word that comes from the mouth of God." In **Jn 4.32-34**, Jesus told His disciples that He had food they didn't know about — which was to do God's will.

So God is our *source* of nourishment and sustenance. When we fast, we're asking God to give us *spiritual* nourishment <u>in place of</u> our *physical* nourishment. And in God's supernatural way, He can even give us the physical energy that we *would have received* from food.

Read Mt 6.16-18.

Does Jesus say, "*If* you fast..." or "*When* you fast..."?
What does this tell us about His expectations for His followers to be fasting?

2) Praying privately.

Read Mt 6.5-6; Lk 6.12.

A prayer closet (or "war room") that's your dedicated place to pray can be very helpful to your prayer life! (The movie *War Room*[1] can be a great inspiration for your private prayer life!) You can put sticky notes up about things to pray for. You can even enhance the space with things that connect you with God — pictures, quotes, sounds, colors, etc. And when you surround yourself with an atmosphere of prayer, it's easier to deepen your prayer life, since there aren't a bunch of other distractions.

A prayer app or other notes app on your phone can be another good place to build your list of what you want to be praying about individually. You can also _set reminders on your phone_ to beep at you daily so you *remember* to take time to pray!

3) Praying corporately.

Just like an in-person friendship, our relationship with God is best when it involves both one-on-one time (personal prayer) and group dynamics with other friends (corporate prayer). Jesus teaches us to do both of these. He instructs us to really seek Him as individuals, *and* really seek Him as a group (corporately).

Read Mt 18.19-20; Acts 1.14.

For praying corporately, I think what Jesus had in mind goes beyond nominating one person to express thanks for a meal or to close out a meeting. Praying together means praying _together_ — as in *collaboration*. It can be organized — or not. It could involve praying Scripture, or praying a song of worship, or kneeling, holding hands, or something altogether different!

But the powerful part of corporate prayer is that...
Hearing prayers can motivate, inspire, and sharpen our own prayers!

Plus you get other people praying in agreement with your prayers — in real time. And vice versa.

Whether we're praying prayers of synchronizing with God or demonstrating His power — regular fasting, "war room" time, and prayer meetings will help us *abundantly* in our growth as disciples who disciple. (Especially the making new disciples part!)

Process Truth

Can you think of someone whose prayer life or prayer style inspires you?
Who and why?

On a scale of 0 to 10, where would you rate your *recent* prayer life?
Why did you rate it that way?

Have you ever tried fasting before? If so, tell us about an experience.

Have you ever participated in a prayer meeting?
If so, what was it like? Could anything make it better?

Do you have a prayer spot or a prayer time?
If so, describe it.
If not, what are your thoughts about those ideas?

Have you ever seen a clear answer to something you prayed? Explain.

What are your thoughts on the following quote?

"Our prayers may be awkward. Our attempts may be feeble.
But since the power of prayer is in the One who hears it and not in the one who says it,
our prayers do make a difference."

– Max Lucado[2]

Apply Truth

To apply this lesson, we're going to challenge one another to fast this week, make plans for prayer for this week, and spend some time praying together before we finish. We'll start with fasting.

Take a moment to set up your fasting plan, and decide when you will apply it this week. Here are some tips...

<u>**How Do I Approach Fasting?**</u>
1) Choose the purpose of your fast:
   • to get in sync with God
   • to ask Him to move in power
2) Choose your type of fast (try 1 of these 2):
   • water only (normal fast)
   • water & juice (If so, read the ingredients and choose juices with no added sweeteners.)
3) Choose the length of your fast (here are some ideas):
   • 2 meals
   • 1 day (including the next night's sleep)
   • 2 or 3 days (if it is your first fast, try 2 days or less)
   • 1 week (FYI, the hardest part of a fast is the first day!)
   • open ended until the purpose is resolved (even up to 40 days!)
4) Eat healthy/light for your last meal leading into your fast
   and your first meal when breaking your fast.
   (You may be tempted to pig out...)
5) Expect:
   • discomfort
   • headache
   • possibility of unusual breath or body odor as your body purges toxins
        (especially for a longer fast — so shower and brush your teeth!)
6) Use your hunger pains/noises as prayer reminders!
   • This is what separates fasting from not eating or simply giving up something.
   • Ask God to give you sustenance and clear focus on Him, along with your main prayer goal.
   • Even if your body doesn't send those physical reminders often,
        spend much more time in prayer than normal during your fast.
7) Drink lots of water so you don't get dehydrated.
8) Fast for God, not for show.
   • Don't brag about fasting (like we already read in Mt 6.16-18).
   • Don't lie about it either.
        Jesus' point in Mt 6 was not to keep it secret at all costs,
        but to stay humble and not come across as "holier than thou."

After you've taken a moment to think through it, **Share your plan with the group.**
If you would like to spend more time thinking or praying about it first, message your group members *within 24-48 hours* with your plan, so they can help you stay accountable this week.

When and how do you plan to spend time in private (prayer closet) prayer?
(This part may or may not overlap with your fasting plan.)

After we conclude this time together, how will you spend time in corporate prayer this week?

Between fasting, praying again in a group, or having some focused private prayer — which do you think will be most challenging to apply this week?

Which are you most excited about applying?

Share Truth

Here are some ideas for bringing this to the next person.
But as Jesus taught in Mt 6, be careful to share this in humility, not pride.

☐ Ask people, "how can I pray for you?" (And write it down so you remember to!)

☐ Invite people to join you in a prayer meeting. Ask to go there together.

☐ Invite a Christian friend to join you in fasting about something you both care about.

What other way(s) might you bring this to the next person?

☐

☐

Pray Corporately

If schedules allow, spend some extra time together in prayer right now. (If not, take note of some of the following ideas to implement at a prayer meeting later this week.) Encourage each member to pray out loud *at least once* during this time. Even if you've never prayed out loud before, developing a *comfort* communicating with God in front of others is vital to growing as His follower. (Imagine if your best friend or significant other refused to speak to you out loud in front of others... How is that different from refusing to pray out loud?)

Don't feel like you need to cover all this list in one sitting, but here are some keywords that may help inspire our prayers. (The lead discipler is welcome to deviate from this and suggest something specific for you to pray about together.)

- closeness
- Kingdom
- forgiveness
- encouragement
- boldness
- justice
- passion
- government

- direction
- Lordship/obedience
- deliverance
- confession
- provision
- compassion
- peace
- church

- praises
- nourishment
- requests
- leadership
- community
- growth
- joy
- family

1 Stephen Kendrick (Producer), & Alex Kendrick (Director), *War Room* (USA; FaithStep Films/Affirm Films/Red Sky Studios/TriStar Pictures, 2015).
2 Max Lucado, *He Still Moves Stones: Everyone Need a Miracle* (Nashville, TN; Thomas Nelson, 2009) 92.

5. Spiritual Lemonade [Stillness]

Pray

Now that we've covered prayer, feel free to be creative in each of the opening and closing prayer times. Mix it up from time to time.

Reflect

Last time we learned about the 2 primary purposes of prayer — to get lined up (synced) with God, and to ask Him to move in power. And we learned the prayer power-ups of fasting, private prayer, and corporate prayer.

How was your experience in corporate prayer this week?

Did you make/find a physical *place* for your private prayer time (if you hadn't before)? How was that?

How was your experience with fasting?

Would there be a strategic part of your regular schedule to overlap fasting with?
E.g. prayer meeting, outreach opportunity, worship service (if people often eat afterward, maybe you could plan to end your fast then), beginning of the month, etc.

What are your thoughts on *continuing* these prayer power-ups?
Will you need *our* help to keep implementing these?

How are we doing with "doing life together?"
Have we done anything outside this meeting time? Do we need to put this next lesson on hold to use this time for dealing with something, or just having some fun together?

Media Placeholder: Spiritual Lemonade

There's nothing like a cold drink when you're warm and thirsty. Whether on a hot summer day, or following some intense physical activity, refreshments such as an ice-cold lemonade refresh *more than* our bodies. Strangely enough, they can actually reach beyond the physical and begin to refresh our attitudes and lift our spirits!

That's because God did not design us as purely *physical* beings. Nor did He design us as purely *spiritual* beings. He weaved body and spirit together so that one affects the other. (That's why fasting works; it repurposing physical discomfort as a spiritual *focusing* tool.)

Both our bodies and our spirits need refreshment! It's easy to tell when our body needs it — and we know what to do about that! But Christians often neglect to refresh our *spirits*. A lot of Christians don't even realize we can *directly* do something about that. Most just settle for bits and pieces of spiritual refreshment as by-products of other activities — like praising God in worship or simply drinking an ice-cold lemonade with thankfulness. But since the main purpose of those other activities is *not* our *spiritual* refreshment, it's very seldom that many Christians ever receive a full dose of that much-needed, deep refreshment.

Even God, who is Spirit, set us an example of being refreshed.

Ex 31.16-17 (ESV) *Therefore the people of Israel shall keep the Sabbath, observing the Sabbath throughout their generations, as a covenant forever.* [17] *It is a sign forever between me and the people of Israel that in six days the Lord made heaven and earth, and on the seventh day he rested and was refreshed.*

So what's the recipe for that soul lemonade? It's a lost art, especially in today's culture. It may be very uncomfortable at first, and may even confront some of our fears. But the return is worth the investment! Without it, we're liable to *try* to do and be all that God wants — while running on empty. Since we *spend* the spiritual energy He gives us, we need to be refueled by God to keep running well.

What we suggest in this lesson may sound instantly refreshing to us (depending on our worship styles). Or it may sound like lemons until we develop some skill in this area and let God bring His sweetness.

[Stillness]

Know Truth

The lost art of making spiritual lemonade has something to do with God's example of being refreshed in **Ex 31.17**. When God rested from His work of creation on the seventh day, He didn't just stop His activity of *work* in order to *switch to* an activity of entertainment or recreation. The Hebrew word for *rest* in **Ex 31.17** (and **Gen 2.2**) is *shavat* (tied to the word *sabbath*). It sends the message that God didn't just switch from one kind of activity to another (like we constantly do in our culture). Instead, He _ceased from_ His activity for that day.

Spiritual refreshment comes through stillness.
Stop and rest.

Read Ps 37.7.

The Hebrew word for "being still" in this passage (*damam*) has to do with *audio* stillness. Be silent before Yahweh.

There's a similar idea of silent stillness in the New Testament.

Read Mark 4.39.

When Jesus told the storm to "be still" —Greek: φιμόω (*phimoō*)— He was telling it to be silenced — even muzzled. The result was a "great calm."

How can we ever *hear from* God if we never turn off our videos, news, or music? How can we ever hear from God —or experience that great calm— if we never stop talking ourselves? Complete stillness tells us to stop the *internal* monologue too, and just *be* before Him.

Spiritual refreshment comes through stillness.
Be silent (inside and out).

Read Ps 46.10.

Rafah. The Hebrew word for "being still" in this verse has to do with letting things alone and loosening our grip. Don't take back control. The old cliche, "let go and let God," flows well with this Hebrew idea.

Spiritual refreshment comes through stillness.
Let go.

There's another Scriptural idea that goes hand-in-hand with stillness. The passages that portray this don't use the words "be still," but you can't really experience stillness without a component of this — *solitude*.

Read Mark 1.35; Mark 6.30-32; John 6.15.

Spiritual refreshment comes through stillness.
Find solitude.

Although our souls *long for* spiritual refreshment, the way to get there messes with our comfort zones and fears.

<u>Stillness involves 4 situations most of us try to *avoid*</u>:
• **Stopping our activity.**
• **Being silent.**
• **Letting go.**
• **Getting alone.**

Let's address these 4 fears.

"Stopping our activity" provokes our Fear Of Missing Out. If I'm not *doing* anything, I'd be missing out on some good entertainment, hanging out with friends, seeing what's happening on social media, or accomplishing something.

But seeking stillness *is* doing something. It detoxes our soul from all our busyness. It's stopping our activity *so that* we can receive the benefit and blessing of rest.

Spiritual refreshment comes through stillness.

"*Being* silent" directly confronts our *fear* of silence. Having constant background noise in our lives (e.g. radio always on in the car, TV always on — even if no one's watching it, earbuds in whenever you're not interacting with someone, etc) actually *trains us* to dislike silence. Noise is a distraction and form of escape that keeps us from thinking too deeply about our *insecurities* or other issues we *should be* dealing with. It's also our biggest obstacle to hearing from God.

Avoiding silence is a self-perpetuating awkwardness. The more we avoid silence, the more we *want to* avoid silence. But since it's a *learned* behavior, we can also *unlearn* it. It's ironic that we *avoid* it, since being silent before God helps to *heal* our insecurities, and opens the door to *hear* from God! God won't always speak to us while we're pursuing Him through stillness; but it opens that door! And that's where we want to be — we just need the courage to endure the awkwardness of noise-withdrawal while we detox our mind. But without that, we'll never be fully renewed.

Spiritual refreshment comes through stillness.

"Letting go" attempts to dethrone our deep idol of *control*. If we're starting to burn out, the idol of control tells us to "just push through it" — which might work in some cases for a while. But we all know that's *not* going to end well. If nothing lets up, the end result will be *complete* burnout, or just trudging through our duties joylessly. Of course our reply to that is, "But if I loosen my grip, things might not go the way *I* want them to…" Control is really a selfishness issue and a trust issue. We don't trust other people —or God— with the outcome *we* want.

But spending time in stillness with God will *prevent*, and even *reverse*, the symptoms of burnout.

It's an exercise in *building* our trust in God. His plan will *always* be better than our plan! Loosening our grip on our striving allows God to replace our anxiety and selfishness with His peace and joy.

Spiritual refreshment comes through stillness.

Finally, **"Getting alone"** may strike fear in some of us because it closely resembles loneliness. This also plays into our insecurities. Being neglected or abandoned is about the worst thing some of us could think of. Fear of being *"left* out" hits us differently from the fear of *"missing* out." *Missing* out has more to do with *degrees* of enjoyment or reward; feeling *left* out has more to do with our *identity*. Being lonely can *feel like* we're *not worth* someone's time or effort.

Others of us might *love to* be alone — because we don't really like people. But that's not what we're going for either! 😉

In solitude, we seek to be alone *with God*. There's a big difference between being *lonely* and being *alone with* someone. They have opposite effects. As Richard Foster wrote in his book, *Celebration of Discipline*, "Loneliness is inner emptiness. Solitude is inner fulfillment."[1] Solitude gives us an opportunity for true one-on-one time with our Creator and Redeemer. In that space, He can build our identity in Him, and just maybe, speak a special direction to us.

Spiritual refreshment comes through stillness.

 Process Truth

On a scale of 1 to 10, how would you rate your level of feeling spiritually refreshed right now?

Have you ever tried the discipline of stillness?

If so, did you experience an awkward/detox/withdrawal period at first? What was that like?

If you made it past the awkwardness, how has God blessed you through stillness?

How frequently do you practice it?

Which aspect of stillness challenges your comfort zones or fears the most? Why?
- **stopping to rest**
- **being silent (inside and out)**
- **letting go**
- **getting alone**

Read Ps 23.1-3a; 1Kings 19.11-13; Isa 30.15,18.
Which of these stillness passages resonates with you the most right now? Why?

 **Apply Truth**

How do we apply an idea that's foreign to most of us?

8 Practical Ideas for Applying the Discipline of Stillness

1) Find a place.
This may be the same as your prayer closet — or maybe not. The best locations for stillness have these traits: a place to find *solitude*, a place that's *peaceful* and relatively free from chatter and artificial sounds, and a place where you can stay *alert*. (Stillness time should not be confused with nap time!) You might search out a handful of places near home, school, and work —even for different seasons— so you'll always be prepared when you need some spiritual refreshment.

2) Keep a notebook or note app handy.
If it's an app, maybe open it and get it set up before you start. (Then set your phone to airplane mode!)
 Sometimes the first thing that pops into our heads when we try to quiet our minds is our To Do list. If that happens to you, jot it down, so you don't have to work at remembering it while you're trying to quiet your mind, and so you don't have to stress about possibly forgetting it! This frees up your brain space! Then when your stillness time is over, you'll be refreshed to work on the list.
 The notebook can also come in handy if you think God might be telling you something during your stillness. Jot it down so you can remember it; then continue in His presence. You can consider it more afterward.

3) Dedicate the time to God.
Start your stillness time with a brief prayer. Offer the time to Him. Ask Him to fill you with His Spirit, His encouragement, and His refreshment. Tell Him you are ready to listen to Him (but realize that He won't speak every time). It's helpful to have the attitude of seeking His *refreshment*, and if He speaks to you — that's a bonus! Then do your best to quiet your mind.

4) Quiet your mind.
This might be the hardest part. Turn off the inner monologue. We constantly think with words and fill the silence in our minds with our own mental chatter. You'll probably interrupt your own stillness many times — especially when you're first starting out! That's okay. When you realize the inner monologue has started back up, just quiet it again.

5) Listen.
Listening can be your best tool for quieting your mind. When we're *truly* listening to a person, we're not talking ourselves. You can use this in your stillness time by listening to the silence. There *will be* ambient noises (unless you're in a sound-proof room). So tune in to any *natural* sounds that are part of God's creation, rather than the noise of machines or people. If there are no natural sounds, then try to tune in to the *white noise* — maybe a fan or distant hum. And listen. The effect is that we're not talking in our head, and we'll have a clear mind in case God does speak to us.

How Does God Speak?
We long to hear an audible voice from God, or hear His message through an angel. "…Like people in the Bible did," we say. Yet even back then, the heroes of the Bible didn't just hear God's voice any time they wanted. It was rare, even for the Prophets to hear God audibly speak. How many times did God speak audibly to Abraham? A handful. To David? A handful. How many times did He give an audible message to Mary or her husband Joseph? A couple. Even if you think the book of the Prophet Isaiah is a really long book — compared to a lifetime of listening for God — what God audibly spoke to him was not a lot.

There are people today who hear God speak with an audible voice, but that is rare — just like in the Bible.

So how does the average disciple "hear" God speak today (besides through His written Word)? Usually, it's a thought that seems to come out of nowhere, that you just "know" is of God. Sometimes it's in your own "voice" (like when you *think* words in your head but don't hear them with your ear), sometimes an image, or idea. We can distinguish it from temptations, distractions, and our own desires in that it lines up with Who we know God to be (through spending time *with Him* and *in His Word*). We will cover more about recognizing and combatting temptation another time.

6) Bask in His refreshment.
Soak it up!

7) Resist the urge to immediately evaluate it and quantify it.
This is also challenging! But just like starting a new exercise program after months (or years) of not exercising — it's *going to feel awkward* at first! But as you develop some skill with it, it will become more natural, and you'll be able reap the fruit of it.

8) Repeat.
If you are really dry, or unaccustomed to stillness, you may need some longer periods of stillness before feeling refreshed. But once you get there, even 5 minutes of stillness per day does wonders to *keep you* spiritually refreshed. You can wait until you bottom out again before applying the discipline of stillness the next time. But why? Working it into our routine can help to keep us fueled and joyful!

Take a moment to think through a plan of how you will approach stillness this week. Things you might consider are: when, where, how long, how often, etc.

Share your plan with one another.

Share Truth

Here are some suggestions of ways to share this with others.

As you try this out…

 share your stillness experiences with a friend or family member outside of this group.
It's good to share about the awkward stages too — just keep them in the loop as you start to develop skill and God begins to fill you or speak to you in new ways.

☐ **Post a verse image or favorite lyric about stillness, rest, or refreshment.**

☐ **When you're with a friend or family member, ask if it's okay to turn off the TV or the car radio.**
Explain that you've been learning about stillness and are looking for ways to remove some of the unnecessary noise from your life.

What other ways might you bring stillness to the next person?

☐

☐

**Pray**

---

1 Richard Foster, *Celebration of Discipline: The Path to Spiritual Growth* (USA; HarperCollins, 1998) 96.

6. Super Soldier [Spiritual Warfare]

Pray

Reflect

Last time we learned that **spiritual refreshment comes through stillness.**
What was your stillness experience like?
> **Was it as challenging or awkward as you expected?**
> **Did you experience fruit from it?**
> **Did you try it more than once?**

How did you bring stillness to someone else?

What about our time with God that *does* involve words?
Any updates about fasting, private & corporate prayer, or your time in the Word?
(Remember that these have all been ways to build our relationship with God — that has been the goal all along!)

> **Did your stillness time affect these other times with God in any way?**

Have you shared the Gospel with someone since we learned how to do that?
> **If so, where are they at with that (as best as you can tell)?**

> **Maybe you've been pouring into a relationship to set that up.**
> **What still needs to happen to make that transition to the Good News?**

Eccl 11.4 (NLT) *Farmers who wait for perfect weather never plant.*
> *If they watch every cloud, they never harvest.*

Is there anything we can do? Maybe pray for a specific individual right now?

Media Placeholder: Super Soldier

In the Marvel Cinematic Universe,[1] we see the character, Captain America, battling countless bad guys — including some very powerful super-humans, aliens, and monsters! Yet that wasn't always the case for Steve Rogers. He started out as a small, sickly, weakling. His passion to defend truth and justice drove him to engage bullies — only to have the snot beat out of him by individuals much stronger than he.

But then he was *transformed* and *equipped* for warfare. When a one-of-a-kind formula was administered to him, Steve was physically transformed into the world's first super soldier! With his new physical stature and super-human strength —and furnished with an indestructible shield— he had the power and protection to engage the enemies of America (and humanity) and defeat them!

Believe it or not, you and I have some things in common with Captain America. One thing is that we both have enemies! *Our* enemies are *spiritual* enemies who will stop at nothing to thwart our cause. Regardless of whether we *know* it or *like* it, there is *always* a battle to be fought because of them.

Another similarity is that, in and of ourselves, we are *powerless* in that battle. Without that super-soldier formula and shield, there's *no way* Steve Rogers could battle those monsters! And *our* enemies (real demons) have both *strength* and *supernatural* power — which basically means they don't fight fairly!

Acts 19.13,15-16 (NIV) *Some Jews who went around driving out evil spirits tried to invoke the name of the Lord Jesus over those who were demon-possessed. They would say, "In the name of the Jesus whom Paul preaches, I command you to come out." …* [15] *One day the evil spirit answered them, "Jesus I know, and Paul I know about, but who are you?"* [16] *Then the man who had the evil spirit jumped on them and overpowered them all. He gave them such a beating that they ran out of the house naked and bleeding.*

Those guys failed because they were neither *transformed* nor *equipped*. But again, like Steve Rogers, we *have* been! As Christians, we're no longer limited to our own feeble strength. We've been given *God's* authority, and *His* power is at work in us! We've also been *equipped* with a shield (and other body armor) — but we need to "suit up" with it. The power and protection is *available* to us as soon as we accept the Gospel — but we have to *train* with it and learn how to engage the enemy. So let's suit up!

[Spiritual Warfare]

Know Truth

Spiritual warfare can be hard to take seriously (or remember) at times, simply because it's an *unseen* battle. But that doesn't make it any less real or serious! We're not talking about cartoonish shoulder angels. We're not talking about being entertained by a fictitious storyline, or suiting up for a costume party. Spiritual warfare involves real, powerful, evil, supernatural beings.

Eph 6.12 (ESV) *For we do not wrestle against flesh and blood, but against the rulers, against the authorities, against the cosmic powers over this present darkness, against the spiritual forces of evil in the heavenly places.*

Our *real* battle is not against people — though it sure seems like it at times! Our *real* battle is against the unseen forces that have been influencing them — demons!

(More precisely, their battle is against us!)

This can open up a whole new worldview about *why* the world is the way it is. And when we learn to suit up for that battle, we can begin to *thwart* the enemy rather than being their unwitting victim time and time again.

A basic first step to battling an enemy is to know who the enemy is. Learning about the backstory of Satan (and the other demons) can help us see why they're against us, and how serious spiritual warfare is. So the following page contains a simple graphic story sequence that sums up where demons came from and why they're our enemy.

Although it's important to not picture our enemy as cartoon characters, a picture can be worth a thousand words…

The Villain's Origin Story

Created as a Glorious Angel

Pride & Violence

Demon

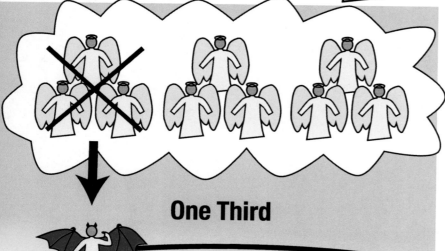

One Third

Jesus didn't become an angel & die for angels; therefore angels aren't offered forgiveness.

Big Grudges!

See Ezek 28.11-17; Isa 14.12-15, Rev 12.3-4a, 7-9, 1Pet 1.12; Heb 2.16-17; 1Cor 6.3

Our enemy has *deep resentment* toward God for casting them out of heaven, and *deep jealousy* of our special favor from God (which they didn't receive). Because of this, **demons are always actively against us**, and **we are told to stay alert!**

Read 1Pet 5.8.

So what should we look for? What are they capable of?
Job 1-2 gives us some very <u>specific examples of the power demons have</u>.

Satan directly…
• stirred up a group of people to rob and murder (**1.15&17**),
• incinerated people with fire from the sky (**1.16**),
• caused a hurricane-force wind that leveled a house full of people (**1.19**),
• and inflicted disease (**2.7**).

To sum that up, **Demons have supernatural power and can plant thoughts.**

Here's a New Testament example of these abilities.

Read Mk 5.2-5.

These demons exerted their supernatural ability through that man by giving him super-human strength. They also convinced him to self-mutilate through cutting. (A tactic that has become a favorite of our enemy in recent years.)

And it's not just "possessed" people that demons have an influence on. Job was a righteous man. The Apostle Paul was tormented by a demon (**2Cor 12.7**). Satan even used the Apostle Peter to tempt Jesus not to go through with His plan of redemption (**Mt 16.21-23**)!

Demons will use their abilities *however they can* to keep non-Christians from experiencing God's forgiveness, and to keep Christians from glorifying God.

So they adapt their tactics to the times and places. In very superstitious cultures, they tend to be more direct and scary, demonstrating their supernatural power to keep people in fear or make them believe in idols. But in a culture like ours, such an overt display of their power (and existence!) would probably send most Americans straight to the church or to their knees!
    Therefore in *our* context, demons are much more *subtle* in their approach.

<u>The tactics of demons include</u> (but are definitely not limited to):
• persuading us that they don't exist (and by extension, that God doesn't either).
• pointing us to anything that distracts us from God — especially to ourselves.
• sowing seeds of distrust about God's commands.
• pitting natural science (which God invented) against faith in a Creator.
• trivializing the seriousness and consequences of sin.
• suggesting that we put our identity in anything but God — even in issues of sin.
• *encouraging* judgment & unforgiveness, and *discouraging* communication.
• keeping us in guilt even after the Holy Spirit has led us to repentance.
• convincing us that *bad decisions* are better than having *no control* in our lives.

Our enemy has been working at their craft for thousands of years and have perfected it. **Demons are masters of deception and distraction!**

Read 1Tim 4.1; 2Cor 11.14-15.

The reason spiritual warfare isn't always obvious is because demons are *really good deceivers*. We wouldn't ever fall for temptation if it didn't look appealing, would we?

Fortunately for us, our God is all-powerful, and our enemy is not! Demons cannot "make" us do anything. Although demons are much stronger than we are (by ourselves), God gives Christians the ability to break their power over us.

Read 1Cor 10.13; 2Cor 10.3-5.

When I recognize that not every thought that flies through my head originated with me, that frees me to evaluate each thought. Then I can either accept it or reject it. When we get to the **Apply Truth** section, we'll look at the specific ways God equips us to battle the enemy.

 Process Truth

Describe how you viewed spiritual warfare before today.
What were the biggest influences that shaped that perspective?

What's been your biggest insight or reminder so far from this lesson?

Does anyone sense they are in the midst of a spiritual warfare situation right now?
How might this realization change your perspective or approach?

Have you ever witnessed the scarier version of spiritual warfare?

Eph 2.1-3 describes 3 sources of our temptations:
the flesh (our own sinful nature), **the world** (media & the influence of culture), and **demons**.

How do we find the balance between not attributing *anything* to demons versus blaming them for *everything bad*?

Not to paint a target on your back, but the fact that we are learning about this right now upsets our enemy. If you haven't felt any spiritual attacks recently, *you just may* in the nearby future. So the **Apply Truth** section will be particularly helpful! (So will making sure we're especially connected with God right now!)

Apply Truth

Our application is to put on the armor God provides. Since it's not a flesh and blood enemy, of course it's not *physical* armor. But the Apostle Paul uses the armor of a Roman soldier as a *mnemonic device* for the ways God equips us for this battle. Each piece is helpful, but when we think through the armor of a Roman soldier, it will help us remember *all* the strategies that together will be very powerful against the enemy. Let's learn to "put on" that armor.

Read Eph 6.10-20.

The Armor of God.

1. Belt — Secure myself in Truth!
A belt holds everything together and gives us stability (like a weight lifting belt). So affirming God's Truth (and continuing to learn and apply it) *stabilizes* us. It helps us *recognize* the enemy's deceptions *as deceptions*. Then we have a much better chance of rejecting them and choosing God's way.

2. Breastplate — Protect my heart by embracing righteousness!
A soldier's chest piece protects their heart and other vital organs in hand-to-hand combat. The illustration here is that when we choose sin, it's like we're exposing our hearts for easier attack. We know from experience that when we choose sin, it becomes easier to *keep* sinning and to sin even *worse*. This can really mess up our emotions! When we're not in the right with God, we're easier prey. But we can protect ourselves by choosing God's way.

But when we do mess up, we can remember our justification — Jesus *declared us righteous!* He overlaid *His righteousness* on ours so that we have no condemnation before God. When we embrace that, we can be quick to repent and restore our *closeness* with God — which again helps protect our heart.

3. Shoes — Be ready to bring the Gospel!

Depending on the translation you use here, v15 might talk about our readiness *from/by* the Gospel (as in NIV/ESV), or our readiness *for* the Gospel (HCSB). Those prepositions (*from*, *by*, or *for*) were actually added as placeholders into our translations. That's because a direct word-for-word translation from the Greek doesn't really follow our normal English sentence structure. It doesn't flow well to say "and having the feet with readiness the gospel the peace." But given that in v19 Paul asks for prayers to proclaim the Gospel, given the Great Commission, and given our enemy's desire to keep people from God, it seems to make the most sense that it's talking about being *ready to share* the Gospel! A verse we looked at in Lesson 2 told us, "…How beautiful are the *feet* of those who bring good news!" (**Rom 10.15**). We are meant to *bring* the Gospel *to others*, not sit contently on it. And when we share that, and people respond to it, we are strengthening our own faith, enlarging God's Kingdom, and directly thwarting the enemy's plans!

4. Shield — Trust God's plan!

The shield Paul describes here was *not* a buckler, the small circular shield a soldier would use in hand-to-hand combat (like Captain America uses). Rather, it was a large door-like shield that was used as cover against a volley of arrows. **Ps 91.4-5** tell us that *God's faithfulness* is also that long shield (and buckler), so we don't need to fear the arrows that fly our way. So *our faith* is in *His faithfulness!* Our faith and trust in God's good plan will shield us and get us through — even when we can't see the outcome yet! God is still in control and He works things out for our good (**Rom 8.28**)!

5. Helmet — Evaluate my thoughts through Christ!

A soldier's helmet obviously protects their head and brain in a fight. Similarly our salvation is the protection for our mind. And our mind is the battlefront of spiritual warfare! When we remember *Whose* we are, and the price He paid to secure our salvation, we won't be tempted to place our identity (and thus our thoughts) in the wrong places. We shouldn't beat ourselves up when an evil thought runs through our head, and we shouldn't link that to our identity! When we remember who we are in Christ, we can take control of our thought life, and take enemy thoughts captive! Between the Helmet of Salvation and the Belt of Truth, we can apply this by *replacing* lies we've accepted (in specific areas of our lives) with God's Truth — over and over until it sticks!

6. Sword — Develop skill with God's Word!

The Bible is our sword. When Jesus was tempted by Satan in the wilderness (**Matt 4 & Luke 4**), He combatted specific temptations with specific Scripture. The more we continue to get God's Word in us, the more familiar and skillful we'll become in wielding it. It can also help to look up passages that deal with the temptations we are most susceptible to, and memorize those passages!

7. Prayer — Pray to suit up!

Apparently Paul couldn't think of a piece of armor that correlated well with prayer. Prayer is like our secret weapon! A very practical way to "put on" the armor of God is to pray through this list in Eph 6. When we do this, we reaffirm the truth of it and regain a godly perspective. It opens our eyes to the deception we're being tempted with, or the way people are being unwittingly used for our enemy's purpose. And remember the mnemonic device — thinking through the standard pieces of armor will help us remember the whole package!

As we went through this armor, did any other practical application ideas come to your mind?

 **Share Truth**

We should use care in sharing this lesson. People don't respond well to being accused of being in league with demons!

And we can't start blaming demons for everything either! Remember that the "world" and our own "flesh" (sinful desires) are sources of temptation too.

But here are some starter ideas to bring this to others.

☐ **Share what you've learned about spiritual warfare with a close friend or family member.**
If it's someone you find yourself getting in unreasonable difficulties with — come up with a mutual code word or phrase that could remind you both that spiritual warfare may be at work. The code word or phrase could be a way to consider that possibility without sounding condemning or accusing in the thick of it.

☐ **Post key verses that remind or inform people of the unseen battle.**

☐ **When you recognize that spiritual warfare is probably at work in someone's situation, offer to pray about it — perhaps praying through the armor of God for them.**

☐ **Encourage friends to read books on spiritual warfare, such as *This Present Darkness*,[2] by Frank Peretti, or *The Screwtape Letters*,[3] by C.S. Lewis, or *Battlefield of the Mind*,[4] by Joyce Meyer.**

Is there anyone new you'd like to bring the Gospel to?
(Remember, this is applying your Gospel shoes!)

☐

☐

What other ways might we bring this awareness or equipping to others?

☐

☐

 **Pray**

Is anyone in the group going through spiritual warfare right now? How about your church/Christian community or its leaders? If so, consider praying through the armor of God on their behalf. Pray for protection, deliverance, encouragement, fruit, clarity.

Pray for your group's spiritual protection now that we are all *in* this battle rather than bystanders.

Now is the time to *make sure* we are connecting with God through His Word, prayer, stillness, worship styles, etc — and that *may be* more challenging than usual this week. Pray for one another in this.

1 Kevin Feige, et al. *Captain America, the First Avenger* (Hollywood, CA; Paramount Home Entertainment, 2011).
2 Frank E. Peretti, *This Present Darkness* (Wheaton, IL; Crossway Books, 2003).
3 C. S. Lewis, *The Screwtape Letters* (USA; HarperCollins, 2001).
4 Joyce Meyer, *Battlefield of the Mind: Winning the Battle in Your Mind* (USA; Warner Faith, 2002).

Part III: BUILDING MOMENTUM

Parts I & II set up a lot of the conceptual pieces of discipleship
— the relational and spiritual aspects.
Part III moves toward beginning to line up our Christian "walk" with Christ,
and gaining some real traction.

7. Huddle [Spirit-Led, Self-Responsible, Team-Supported]

Pray

Reflect

Last time, we opened our eyes to the unseen battle that's constantly unfolding around us. We learned that demons use their abilities however they can to keep non-Christians from experiencing God's forgiveness, and to keep Christians from glorifying God.

Did the last lesson change your perspective of any situations you witnessed or experienced since then? If so, how?

Did you find a particular reason to pray through the Armor of God this week (for yourself or someone else)? Or looking back, was there a situation where that would've been helpful?

Did you have beautiful feet this week? (Did you bring the Gospel to anyone?)

How was your time with God this week?

Do we need any renewed accountability?

Media Placeholder: Huddle

When a sports team works together as a unit, it's a beautiful thing.

No single person is completely responsible for the end result of a game. A coach will give direction and motivation — but it's the players on the field who pull off the plays — or not. Even when one player has a particularly excellent play, that play is set up and made possible by the rest of the team.

In football, it's not just the coach's guidance, or the quarterback's throw… It's the center's snap, all the blockers, multiple receivers getting into position — and all *continuing through the play*, and making adjustments based on the opposing team's movements. An individual could potentially sabotage the play by not doing their part. But one person can't make it happen all by themselves. It's a team sport.

Church is like a team sport too! Each of the players needs to be communicating and working together — following through and making adjustments along the way.

Eph 4.15-16 (NIV) *Instead, speaking the truth in love, we will grow to become in every respect the mature body of him who is the head, that is, Christ.* ¹⁶ *From him the whole body, joined and held together by every supporting ligament, grows and builds itself up in love, as each part does its work.*

God is the Head of the body; Head Coach of the church team. And the members of the body/team need to be following the Coach's lead. They can't be dropping the ball for lack of investment. Each member needs to pull their own weight — not as an individual apart from the team, but collaborating *with* the team.

The more players there are who are *invested in the teamwork of a specific team* — the more the church will *experience wins*.

When a *church* team works together as a unit, it's a beautiful thing! It builds camaraderie. It builds excitement. It builds momentum. And when most of the team starts doing this, the church will start playing like champions for their Coach!

[Spirit-Led, Self-Responsible, Team-Supported]

 **Know Truth**

As disciples of Jesus, God wants us to be
Spirit-led, self-responsible, and team-supported.

Many Christians tend to zero in on *one* of these within their own walk.

- Some of us seek to be Spirit-led — but to a *fault* in that we're afraid to make a move without a billboard from God! *Or* we tend to "rely on the Spirit" as an excuse for not preparing well.

- Some of us are self-responsible go-getters — but at the *expense* of regularly waiting or listening for God, or enlisting help from the rest of the team.

- Some of us like the team to take care of *us!* We like being well-fed and served — in fact, we kind of *expect* that. But somehow we're usually too "busy" when there's opportunity for *us* to invest back the other way.

It's challenging to live in balance of all three. So let's take a look at God's design for each piece.

Spirit-Led

Read Rom 8.5; Gal 5.16-17,25.

So how do we do that?
How do we know what the Holy Spirit wants, in order to stay in line with Him?

Back in Lesson 1, we read in **2Pe 1.21** that Bible authors "spoke from God as they were carried along by the Holy Spirit." Also, in last week's lesson, we read **Eph 6.17**, which told us that God's Word is the "sword of the Spirit." So on a very straightforward level…

• The Holy Spirit speaks to us through the Bible.

As Christians, *if* we're getting God's Word in us, we'll *know* where we're in line with the Spirit, and where we're not. When we're reading the Bible and our heart is suddenly poked, and we realize we're not in line with what it's telling us — consider that poke a direct invitation by the Holy Spirit to make a change!
Do something about it! Follow the Coach's instruction.

• The Holy Spirit also speaks to us directly.

In the Apply Truth section of Lesson 5, we learned how God speaks. Within the Trinity, this is generally the role of the Holy Spirit. The Spirit *does* speak through dreams, visions, or an audible voice (**Acts 2.17; Acts 10.19; Acts13.2; Heb 4.7**). But *much more frequently*, He speaks by inserting a thought that we just *know* is from God — and quite possibly outside our comfort zone! The more we obey that voice, however, the *less un*comfortable we'll be with following it.

Self-Responsible

It was our own decision and responsibility to personally accept the Gospel and become disciples. Likewise, it's our individual responsibility to *grow as disciples*. It's the Spirit's job to lead us and sanctify us. And fellow members of the church are supposed to encourage us, challenge us, and serve alongside us. But if we're not *active, willing participants*, we'll never experience real growth or maturity ourselves!

There are two pieces to this. Whether you've realized this or not, the first one has been the focus of the entire first half of this training.

• I am responsible for growing my relationship with God.

It's not realistic for me to expect to *continue growing* as a disciple, *beyond this curriculum*, if I'm not learning to "feed myself" along the way. Accountability, like we've been trying to implement, can be a very helpful *supplement to* a heart for God. But tuning my heart, establishing healthy habits (spiritual disciplines), and asking friends to help keep us on track — those responsibilities lie with me.

Beyond this group, the community of church is meant to bless us and enhance our relationship with God. But what if our worship leader or pastor are recruited by a megachurch — or experience a massive moral failure? What if we get a job and move to another city? We need to set ourselves up for long-term success in our *own ability* to be filled by, and submit to, our Lord.

Read Heb 5.11-14.

"Baby" Christian is a term for a brand new Christian who's recently been reborn. Christians might stay at that baby level for only weeks or months… or for decades. That's why we have to take responsibility for our own Christian maturity. Instead of viewing church as our mommy who always feeds us milk, we need to be *seeking out* the ingredients of the Bible, prayer, worship styles, stillness, etc, and put together the combination that will keep us fueled by God. Our continued *responsiveness* and *obedience* to the Spirit is also a core part of that maturing process.

The second piece of our responsibility is this…

• I am responsible for doing my part in the church.

In his book, *I Am a Church Member*,[1] Thom Rainer warns against a country club mentality when it comes to church membership. People join a country club for all the perks, and to be served by others. But as members of the church, we need to serve and support *one another*!

Read Gal 5.13; Eph 4.15-16.

Each part needs to do its work. In a later lesson, we'll dig deeper into the topic of *service*, and where and how we might serve in specific ways. But the point here is to wrap our minds around the idea of having a *responsibility to* the church. This goes beyond our sense of community and belonging. It was never God's intention for a church's staff and core leaders to do all the work of ministry while the members sit back and soak it all up. We are all meant to be *active participants*. Collaborators.

Team-Supported

Though we're meant to be responsible, that doesn't mean we should work alone. The team can help us in a couple big ways.

• The team is meant to help relieve our struggles, pain, and weaknesses.

Read Gal 6.2; Php 4.12-14.

Our team can relieve burdens. They can help us through rough personal times.

That is uncomfortable for many of us — but it's God's design. Our Christian community is meant for *more* than a source of friendship. It's meant to *help* us. And vice versa. So we need to *let* our team share our burdens.

This ends up blessing the ways we serve the church individually, because we won't be so distracted or overwhelmed by our burdens.

The other big way we're meant to be team-supported is in our ministry.

• The team is meant to share the work of ministry and expand it.

Some of us are those go-getters who tend to be really good at being self-responsible. If so, we may have a hard time asking for help. It may be that we *don't want* help; or maybe we're just *too busy serving* to think about recruiting others. But consider this example in the early church.

Read Acts 6.1-7.

When the first real need (and opportunity) arose in the church, the Apostles didn't just say, "Let's add this to our plates too!" Instead, they recruited help. Verse 3 points out that they didn't even take on the task of choosing these seven food administrators themselves. They let the church members choose among themselves (thus encouraging self-responsibility).
  What was the big-picture result in verse 7? The Gospel spread more rapidly!

Recruiting the help of fellow teammates not only expands our ministry, but it frees us up to be more effective in the way *we* serve! And it blesses the church's ministry as a whole!

There is quite a bit of overlap between being Spirit-led, self-responsible, and team-supported. And that makes sense, since God designed the disciple's life to intertwine all three!

Read 1Cor 3.6-10.

To sum it up…**We're responsible to <u>do our part</u> to <u>partner with God</u> and <u>with His team</u>.**

Process Truth

What does following God's leading look like when it's not something directly from the Bible? Here's an example to consider.

Read Acts 8.29-31,35-36.

Whether it was by vision, audible words, or a thought — it doesn't really matter. What matters is that Philip knew God wanted him to go up to the chariot.

How did Philip initially respond to the Holy Spirit's leading?

Did the Spirit give him step by step instructions after that?

How did Philip know what to do after he got to the chariot?
What are the implications for us?

Where is your progress in developing long-term habits for growing your relationship with God? Consider where you *used* to be, where you *want* to be, and where you're *at*.

Do we need to bump up our accountability in any specific area to help establish those healthy habits?

Is your natural tendency toward initiative or passivity?
Has this affected your ministry involvement? How so?

Do you find it challenging to let others help you?
Would your answer be the same for both ministry/work, and moral support?
Why do you think you feel that way?

Apply Truth

Spirit-Led

How do we know a thought is from God, and not just something we want, or even a temptation? One confirmation is that...

The Holy Spirit will *never* tell us something contrary to His written Word!

Sorry to disappoint, but God will never choose our "happiness" over our obedience. God wants us to use discernment —not feelings— in evaluating the ideas we think may be from Him.

Read Rom 12.2; 1Th 5.19-22.

How do we *test* those thoughts?
We can ask questions like these: (Note they're not all in the positive!)
• Does it line up with God's Word?
• Does it make sense according to *godly* wisdom or God's character?
• Is there any long-term or eternal significance to it?
• Will it use my gifts or abilities?
• Will it distract me from a higher priority God has called me to?
• Will it stretch/grow me?
• Will it bless others?
• And if it passes the other tests (and it kind of seems like a bigger decision)...
     Do I have an excitement (maybe nervous excitement) about it?

Self-responsible

As was mentioned, we'll focus on the topic of *service* in a later lesson. But what if I really want to get started helping, and have no idea where to begin? Here's a starting point.

Sometimes someone will come up to their pastor or ministry leader and say, "I'd like to help; I'd like to get more involved." The leader asks them, "In what area would you like to do that?" If they say, "I don't know..." or "I'll do anything," the leader may be thinking of 20 different needs or ideas — or they might not be able to come up with anything on the spot because they're so used to doing everything themselves.
     But if the member says, "I'll do anything," the church leader might say, "Okay, I'd like you to come up with a new publicity flyer every couple weeks." Well what if that member has no eye for design? What if they're asked to be a greeter, but have no social skills? What if they're asked to balance the sound board, but are tone deaf?

It's *much more helpful*, if we take the initiative to look around at the ministry. Not just a glance, but study it for a week or two, or a month, and pay attention to the behind-the-scenes things. Think about the parts that you know *somehow happen*, but you aren't sure how they get done. When we do this, **we can observe where ministry intersects our abilities and interests!**

We may spot something that's being done, and think, "I could *help* with that!" Or we may see an area that's struggling with some mismatched volunteers, and think, "I could *develop* that, or even *lead* that!" Or we may see something that's *missing* and gain a *vision* to serve in a new way, or meet a new need. Part of our responsibility is recognizing where we could be of service, and taking initiative. But it takes that first step of noticing.

Willingness is appreciated. But willingness and a rough idea of abilities and wiring is much better! For example, "I enjoy administrative tasks," or "I love working with my hands," or "I really like working with video," or "I'd love to take someone else through this curriculum." 😉

Team-Supported

What do you think?
What *action step* could you take to recruit the kind of support that's most needed in your life or ministry right now?

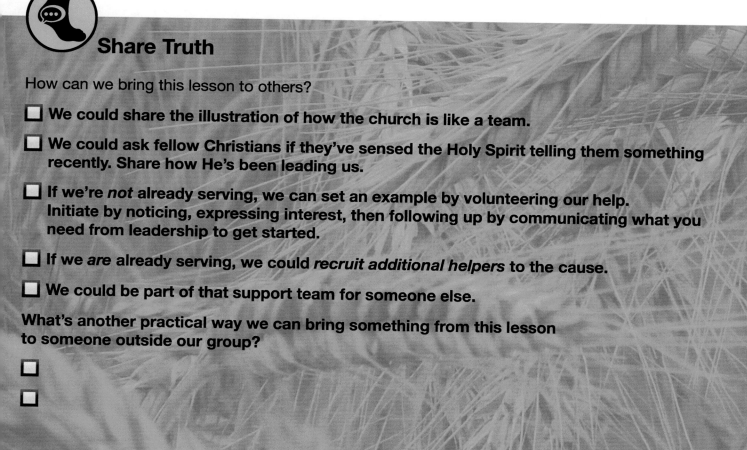

Share Truth

How can we bring this lesson to others?

☐ **We could share the illustration of how the church is like a team.**

☐ **We could ask fellow Christians if they've sensed the Holy Spirit telling them something recently. Share how He's been leading us.**

☐ **If we're *not* already serving, we can set an example by volunteering our help. Initiate by noticing, expressing interest, then following up by communicating what you need from leadership to get started.**

☐ **If we *are* already serving, we could *recruit additional helpers* to the cause.**

☐ **We could be part of that support team for someone else.**

What's another practical way we can bring something from this lesson to someone outside our group?

☐

☐

**Pray**

Huddle time. Team (corporate) prayer seems fitting.

---

1 Thom S. Rainer, *I Am a Church Member: Discovering the Attitude that Makes the Difference* (USA; B&H Publishing Group, 2013) chapter 1.

8. Masks [Integrity]

Pray

Reflect

Last time we learned about being Spirit-led, self-responsible, and team-supported.

Have you sensed the Holy Spirit speaking to you or prompting you about anything this week?
   If so, describe it.
   If not, did you take any opportunities to *invite Him* to speak?

Were there any situations (especially spiritually) this week, when you were tempted to be passive, but still chose to take responsibility for yourself?

How have you let fellow Christians come around you to support you in any new ways, with either personal help or ministry/serving help?

Did any situations pop up this week that you thought could be spiritual warfare?
   If so, did it lead you to take any specific action (including praying about it)?
   Did you notice any change afterward?

How are your personal spiritual disciplines going? Has there been anything especially refreshing or insightful from your time with God?

Media Placeholder: Masks

Ancient Greek theatre dates back about 5 centuries *before* the time of Jesus. During performances, the actors wore masks to help them step into character. Scripts were written to include only 2-3 actors in total, but more *characters* could be introduced to the story by switching masks. A quick costume and mask change allowed an actor to enter the stage in multiple roles without the audience necessarily knowing who the individual actor was.

With the right mask and wardrobe, an actor could play a variety of characters —young or old, male or female— even within the same performance. (They only allowed male actors at the time.) Whatever the playwright and audience wanted — the actor just needed to memorize the right lines and put on the right mask.

In Greek, an actor like this was called a *ὑποκριτά* (hupokrita).This is where we get the English word *hypocrite*.

According to the *New Oxford American Dictionary*,[1] hypocrisy is "the practice of claiming to have moral standards or beliefs to which one's own behavior does not conform."

So a hypocrite is someone who portrays a standard that does not match who they really are. Kind of like being an actor — or wearing a mask. This connotation for the Greek word for actor has been used for a long time. Jesus even used it.

Matt 23.27-28 (ESV) *"Woe to you, scribes and Pharisees, hypocrites! For you are like whitewashed tombs, which outwardly appear beautiful, but within are full of dead people's bones and all uncleanness. [28] So you also outwardly appear righteous to others, but within you are full of hypocrisy and lawlessness.*

Living as a disciple of Jesus *isn't* about appearances. It's *not* about saying the right things around the right people. It's *not* about *stepping into the right character* for the right environment.

Living as a disciple is about *building righteous character* into our lives through the sanctifying power of the Holy Spirit. It's about being the same person with the same standards — whether on or off the stage. It's about striving to make our words, actions, and beliefs *consistently* line up. In other words it's about *integrity!*

[Integrity]

Know Truth

Many people today "switch hats" to try to *conform to* the crowd they're with — and also to *impress* them. They may put on the "intellectual" hat for school, the "wild and crazy" hat for parties, and the "pious, I-have-everything-together" hat for church. They make their life about *convincing*, rather than *becoming*. They spend their time *convincing others* that they're *already* the person they *should be* (according to that group's standards).

But as *apprentices*, we should spend our time *becoming* who God *created us to be!*

In **Gen 1.26-27**, it says that God created mankind in His image. Humanity was created to resemble God's likeness (more so in *character* than physical features). Then that image was tainted in **Gen 3** when Adam and Eve chose to sin. But God had already laid out a plan to reclaim His image through Jesus and the Gospel.

When people are reborn as Christians, God *re*-creates us in His image.

Read Eph 4.22-24; Rom 8.29.

It is the *destiny* of Christians to be conformed back to the likeness of God! That means righteousness, integrity, and character. It's *going to happen* sooner or later — God would just rather it happen *sooner*, with our cooperation!

God's plan to line my character up with His isn't just about me. It *does* benefit me, but it's *not just* for my benefit. This is bigger than us. It's about His plan for the world!

Read 2Cor 5.17-21.

This is kind of a deep passage, and we're going to break it down a bit. So just say so if you'd like us to reread it for comprehension first…

When we became a "new creation" (v17), we started becoming the "righteousness of God" (v21). Jesus *declared us* righteous when we initially became Christians. But then it's that life-long process of *sanctification* through the Holy Spirit that brings our lives in line with that. All this is for the *purpose* of being ambassadors of reconciliation (v18-20). As Christians, we personally represent the King (as His ambassadors) in sharing His Gospel (the message of reconciliation).

Therefore, if we're not *demonstrating* or *becoming* the "righteousness of God" —meaning our integrity and character are not where they need to be— we'll be poor witnesses, and therefore ineffective in our mission!

Hypocrisy is one of the biggest detriments to the spread of the Gospel!

Mohandas K. Gandhi was quoted as saying, "I like your Christ, I do not like your Christians. Your Christians are so unlike your Christ."

Dr. Phil Pringle, in his book, *Top 10 Qualities of a Great Leader*,[2] describes an incident that permanently scarred Gandhi's views of Christianity. Pringle included this story in a list of blown opportunities.

After growing up in India and attending law school in England, as a young man, Gandhi began practicing law in South Africa. Gandhi had started to read the New Testament, and in particular, he loved Jesus' Sermon on the Mount teaching in **Mt 5-7**. At a stage in his life when he seemed to be a seeker, he attempted to attend a particular church one Sunday. A white South African elder of the church labeled Gandhi (who was a dark-skinned Indian) by a racial slur, and barred his entrance to worship. That church hypocrite single-handedly closed the door of true Christianity in Gandhi's life.

But what if that church elder had actually been a *new creation* in Christ?
What if he'd been *discipled* according to God's Word,
was working on his *personal integrity*,
and was actively pursuing the *Great Commission*?
Perhaps through him or that church, the Holy Spirit would have opened Gandhi's eyes to the Truth of the Gospel.
Perhaps instead of his human-powered work of non-violence (inspired by Jesus' teaching to "turn the other cheek" in **Mt 5.39**), Gandhi *may* have had Holy Spirit power to speak the Gospel to the many millions he ended up influencing across India and the world!
But as it happened, Gandhi never grew to see Jesus as more than an inspirational moral teacher after that encounter. He never entered into a relationship with the Son of God Who was the only One Who could have taken away his sins. Hypocrisy is one of the biggest detriments to the spread of the Gospel!

So it's not about switching hats or masks to fit the crowd!

Read Prov 10.9.

If I'm trying to live a double-life —trying to *veer off* the straight path at certain places without my church friends knowing it— I'll eventually be found out. But this proverb says there's *security* in walking with integrity. We'll have a lot more *peace* (and a lot less anxiety) if we're not trying to hide things!

Read Luke 16.10.

If I don't have integrity about *little* things, I can't be trusted to have integrity about *big* things — whether with my money, with my words, or with my actions. So this tells us we *cannot realistically confine* a "little" dishonesty or a "little" immorality to a certain corner of our lives! It will eventually grow — either deeper and deeper within that one area, or it will spread to other areas of our lives.

If I have integrity, I will have it regardless of the situation at hand!

Whether a big issue or little issue, whether public or private — integrity is integrity. The late John Wooden (Basketball Hall of Fame player and coach) said this about character:

"Be more concerned with your character than with your reputation. Your character is what you really are while your reputation is merely what others think you are." — John Wooden[3]

Integrity shows what a person *is*, not just what they want others to *believe* about them. And this is crucial to living as an apprentice of Jesus!

Process Truth

A concept the world pushes at times is this: "It's okay to do the wrong thing for the right reason."

Would a person of integrity follow this philosophy? Explain.

Consider the following *integrity* grading scale:
"A" — consistent through and through in word, deed, and thoughts
"B" — slightly working the system to give others an inflated impression
"C" — average: honest and faithful in some areas, but not in others
"D" — a little worse than the average person
"F" — failing at personal integrity; I'm not at all who I claim to be

Based on this scale, how would you grade your *personal integrity* over the past couple months?

Read Matt 15.8.

In a human relationship, what happens to the *closeness* of that relationship when we *say* one thing, but regularly *show* the opposite?

If someone does this with God (saying one thing, but doing another), should they expect to experience real *closeness* or *fruit* in their relationship with Him?

In which area of life do you find yourself *most tempted* to deviate from what you say, or to mislead others about what's really going on?
　　　Can you identify the reason why that tempts you?

Apply Truth

Read Titus 2.6-8.

Paul was instructing Titus in discipleship! You may have started your own discipleship group with this curriculum by now — or maybe that opportunity is still ahead of you. But keep in mind that God wants us to lead others to Him, and train them in a solid foundation, so that *they* can continue the apprenticing movement too! This keeps His kingdom growing — and multiplies it!

And as disciplers (and future disciplers), much of our witness rests on our integrity. Paul instructs Titus (and by extension, us) to set an example in both our actions and our words. This gives us credibility for the people God wants us to influence — whether with younger disciples or with seekers.

Read Matt 5.14-16.

**The point of integrity is not to make *us* look good,
but to make *God* look good to the people around us!**

And if we live with integrity, we <u>will</u> make God look good!

Integrity *starts* with the *desire* to want to do good. That doesn't mean we'll carry that out perfectly every time, but it starts with that desire. The Apostle Paul shared his struggles with this in **Rom 7**. It's a great read (and kind of deep)! As new creations in Christ, we are released from *slavery* to sin. We are released from the *law* of sin. So we possess a *freedom* and *potential* to overcome sin, that we did not possess before knowing Christ.

But the choice remains with us! We *don't have to* submit to sin anymore! In each situation, we can choose the temptation, or choose to line up with the Holy Spirit. Integrity is about lining up our thoughts, words, and actions with the righteousness the Holy Spirit is calling us to. It's letting God sanctify us!

**Integrity *starts* with a <u>desire</u> to do good,
but *takes effect* through our <u>words</u> and <u>actions</u>.**

How do we apply this? What are the specifics?

In our <u>words</u>...

• **Integrity looks like honesty.**
   (Eph 4.15; Col 3.9-10)

• It does **not** look like **deception** (including "white lies" or misdirection).
   (Acts 5.1-11)

• It does **not** look like **crude language**.
   (Eph 5.4; Col 3.8)

• It does **not** look like **gossip**.
   (2Cor 12.20)

If I'm a person of integrity, I'll strive to have my words consistently reflect who I am in Christ. If people heard every word, and knew every relevant detail, they should have no reason to question my integrity. As we read earlier, this is what Paul instructed Titus.

In our _actions_...

• **Integrity looks like practicing what we preach.**
> (Matt 23.1-3,25-26)

• It looks like **following through** and **keeping our word**.
> (Matt 5.33-37, Matt 21.28-31)

• It looks like **obeying our Lord** whom we pledged ourselves to.
> (John 14.15, Luke 6.46)

There is no magic formula for applying integrity, other than gaining God's perspective of it and choosing it.
> There is a big difference between a saved person who dismisses certain sins as "unimportant," versus an apprentice who wants their life to glorify God in every way.

Col 3.17 (NIV) _And whatever you do, whether in word or deed, do it all in the name of the Lord Jesus, giving thanks to God the Father through him._

Share Truth

We encounter many people whose lives we have no voice in. If there is no relationship there, "correcting" them will often turn them away from God rather than drawing them to Him. But here are some ideas of what we _can_ do.

In our own lives,

☐ **following through or doing the right thing when that involves sacrifice will speak volumes to those watching us!**

☐ **In love, speak into the lives of the Christians around you;**
• hold them to their word,
• call them into account,
• and when their words reflect crudeness, gossip, or blasphemy, call it out.

Be careful to distinguish born-again Christians from church-goers or "nominal" Christians who have not yet responded to Jesus. We should not expect non-Christians and seekers to live up to God's standards (or to care about that).

☐ **In love, hold coworkers and classmates to their word.**
If they have a responsibility that they are not upholding, ignoring it and letting it slide will do them no favors in life. Don't be self-righteous about it, but humbly encourage them to follow through on

what they say, since that quality will be useful to their future.

☐ **Promote honesty and integrity.**
Post about them. Talk about them. They are good character values that will benefit anyone. Being the light is more effective than kicking the darkness!

☐ **Apologize** for being hypocritical or fake ourselves. Ask for accountability.

What's another way we can bring this lesson to the next person?

☐

☐

Pray

1 Angus Stevenson and Christine A. Lindberg, editors, *New Oxford American Dictionary*, 3rd ed (Oxford University Press, 2010).
2 Phil Pringle, *Top10 Qualities of a Great Leader* (USA; Harrison House Publishers, 2008) 68-69.
3 John Reger, *Quotable Wooden: Words of Wisdom, Preparation, and Success By and About John Wooden, College Basketball's Greatest Coach* (USA; Taylor Trade Publishing, 2012) 65.

9. Shackles [Removing Idols]

Pray

Reflect

How are you doing, *really*?
Last time, we talked about integrity versus hypocrisy, so don't just answer "good" if it's not. Share with your team how you're *really* doing. We can spend as much time here as needed, and postpone the lesson if that would be helpful.

Since we met last time, have you <u>*recognized*</u> any opportunities to choose integrity when <u>*tempted*</u> to fudge the truth or cheat on something?
    If so, how did you do with that temptation?

Has our enemy turned up the heat since we talked about spiritual warfare?

How is your personal time with God going with the Word, prayer, fasting, stillness, and worship style? (Remember that these disciplines are our foundations for connecting with God and being able to apply anything else.)

Where are we at with discipling others?
If you've started a group, where is that at and how is it going?
If you haven't started a group, what are your thoughts?
Do you need encouragement or anything else from us?

Media Placeholder: Shackles

Human trafficking has become a global problem. Modern day slavery. It's kind of unbelievable that it still exists, but it does! Human souls are sold for sex or sold for physical labor. Some are drugged or kidnapped when they thought they were making a new friend or interviewing for an "off the books" job. Others are even sold out by parents! It's horrifying!

But it's not just "over there," across the sea. It's here in America, in our state, and probably in our closest medium to large sized city. For decades, the problem was either unknown, or ignored. But with the first *Taken* movie, and with the spread of the *End It Movement* (and similar causes), the American public has been taking notice, spreading awareness, and paving the way for rescue stories.

God *loves* rescue stories! (He invented them!) He desires His creation to live in freedom. Listen to what God spoke through the prophet Isaiah about the coming Messiah:

Isaiah 42.6-8 (HCSB) *"I, Yahweh, have called You for a righteous purpose,*
and I will hold You by Your hand.
I will keep You and appoint You to be a covenant for the people
and a light to the nations,
⁷ in order to open blind eyes, to bring out prisoners from the dungeon,
and those sitting in darkness from the prison house.
⁸ I am Yahweh, that is My name;
I will not give My glory to another or My praise to idols.

God wants to set His people free from darkness and bondage!

There's *another* form of bondage existing today, which is even more rampant than human trafficking. It's the prison of *idolatry!* Regrettably, it can keep even born-again Christians bound and unfruitful. Of course, with this kind of idolatry, we're not talking about the worship of carved images. Rather, it's about issues in our lives that we've allowed to resonate with us more deeply than God does — and they end up keeping us in bondage.

If *sin* is the shackle binding us to the dungeon wall, and the *Gospel* is what frees us from that shackle, then *idolatry* is like putting our hand back into the loosened cuff and holding on to the chain!

[Removing Idols]

Know Truth

Let's unpack this paradox of being spiritually free, yet still in bondage to sin. It sounds kind of ridiculous! Yet anyone who's been a Christian very long probably knows this from experience.

Romans 6-8 is a great (and lengthy) passage about this continuing struggle between freedom and bondage. Even the apostle Paul continued to wrestle with sin after becoming a Christian! Paul —the apostle, evangelist, and missionary who wrote most of the New Testament— wrestled with sin as a Christian too!

In the introduction to this passage, **Rom 6.1-7** says that when we were baptized, we officially died to our old selves. We officially died to sin and were released from its bondage.
> Yet... sin is still a factor. Why is that?

Read Rom 6.13-16.

Paul explains that though we are free in Christ, if we offer ourselves back to sin, sin will gladly take us up on that offer! It's not bondage at the _eternal soul_ level anymore (because we were completely _justified_), but only at the _practical daily living_ level now (because we're still being _sanctified_).

Quick review:
What's the difference between justification and sanctification?

In **Rom 7.14-20**, Paul shares his frustration with his *personal* struggle with sin. Then he sums up that wrestling...

Read Rom 7.21-8.2.

Paul didn't make *excuses* for sin; but he acknowledged that *the struggle is real!*
> Yet he *wasn't content* in that struggle! He didn't have a *defeatist* attitude that sin would *always* be his master. If he *had*, it wouldn't have been much of a "struggle!"

But then he shared *his rescue story*! He thanked God (the Father), and attributed his ongoing deliverance to both Jesus Christ and the Holy Spirit.

So what does the ongoing struggle with sin have to do with *idolatry*?

Idolatry is the reason we have a continuing struggle with any sin.

In 1Corinthians, Paul connects common temptation to idolatry.

Read 1Cor 10.6-8,11-14.

Paul was referring to Israel's incident with the golden calf idol in **Exodus 32**. But as he's addressing *Christians* about idolatry, he didn't mention the calf idol statue itself. Rather, he connected idolatry to the unrestrained pursuit of pleasure.

Then he talked about God providing an escape route from each *temptation*, and brought it back around to fleeing from idolatry.

Idolatry is the reason we have a continuing struggle with any sin.

But it's not just something we have to be stuck with! Paul assures the Corinthians that God provides that way out! We will get into the *how* of that in the *Apply Truth* section. But before we get there, it's helpful for us to specifically identify what we're up against.

There are countless idols we could identify in people's lives today. We might recognize them as sinful habits, as fears that drive us, or as major life imbalances — whatever we put above God. Yet they *all* seem to stem from a few core issues. The Authentic Manhood[1] movement identifies 3 "deep idols," which are the roots that all the other "surface idols" grow from. Here's an adaptation of those.

3 Deep Idols

The Control Idol
This idol tells us that everything will be okay and secure if we can just gain some element of control or power in a situation. It plays into our finances, schedules, accomplishments, and relationships. It tells us that the outcome is always up to us. This idol promises happiness through stability and power. It feeds on the fear that we're powerless or that something bad will happen if we don't intervene. If we have this idol in our lives, we're generally tempted by things that make us feel like we can have control, power, or stability.

The Significance Idol
This one tells us we'll be important or worthy if only we can gain the approval of a particular group — coworkers, friends, family members, etc. We'll go to any lengths to impress, or to save face. This idol promises happiness through affirmation and acceptance. It preys on the fear that we're worthless unless we convince people otherwise. If we have this idol in our lives, we're generally tempted by things that make us feel important or special.

The Comfort Idol
The third deep idol tells us that life is good only when we're having fun! Life should be easy, and therefore responsibility and hard work are things to be avoided. Thrills, entertainment, and relaxation rule our time, energy, and money. This idol promises happiness through pleasure, often at the expense of the long term picture. It feeds on the Fear Of Missing Out. If we have this idol in our lives, we are generally tempted by fun — and we'll worry about the consequences later.

It's *not* that experiencing security, acceptance, or pleasure are bad. God *wants* all of those for us — just *not* at the expense of our love and obedience for *Him*. Bryan Carter, from Authentic Manhood, expressed it this way. He said, "Idols come from legitimate desires that are being expressed in inordinate or inappropriate ways."[2]

Process Truth

Consider this short list of sins, stronghold fears, or life imbalances that might be considered "surface idols." Discuss which "deep idols" could possibly be the root behind each one. (There may be more than one deep idol that could explain it!)

- Cheating on a test

- Sexual impurity

- Bitterness

- Sports obsession

- Stinginess

- Gossip

Which of the three *deep* idols do you identify with the most?
Take a moment and reflect on why that may be.
(Was there an environment or situation from your past that may have helped shape this?)

Bryan Carter, from Authentic Manhood, said, "The noble fight against sin and temptation is not just about behavior modification. Behavior modification without heart change is dangerous."[3]

Have you ever tried to stop surface idols by shear will power?
If so, how effective was that?

What might be the *dangers* of setting rules and trying harder, then failing?

What might be the *dangers* of setting rules and trying harder, then seeming to succeed (at least temporarily)?

Sometimes we are actively aware of idols we are still in bondage to.
Sometimes we have blind spots with our idols.
Sometimes we are aware of our tendencies toward idolatry,
and because of that we are "careful" or "take heed" as Paul instructed in **1Cor 10.12**.
Which of these describes your current situation with idols and strongholds?

 **Apply Truth**

Gal 5.1 (ESV) *For freedom Christ has set us free; stand firm therefore, and do not submit again to a yoke of slavery.*

Jesus paid a high price for our freedom! He wants us to *experience* that freedom in full! Not just the salvation part, but also the daily living part! Paul tells us not to submit to bondage again. It's for *freedom* that Christ has set us free! Therefore…

Don't be trafficked by the empty promises of idols!

But how can we *avoid* that?
What alternative is there to simply trying harder?
We can set up healthy boundaries and ask for accountability — which can be very helpful in this freedom battle. But if that's the crux of our strategy, it kind of falls into the category of rules and trying harder. It may be helpful in changing the behavior for a while, but it doesn't *fix* the core problem!

Listen to the common theme provided by these authors and presenters.

"Crucifying the [flesh] is about strangling sin at the motivational level, rather than simply setting ourselves against sin at the behavioral level."[4] — **Timothy Keller**

"Remember: getting free isn't about jumping through the right hoops or correcting your thinking. Freedom comes from a changed heart and a fundamental belief that God is good and intends good things for you…"[5] — **Brian Tome**

"Instead of trying to conquer sin by working hard to change our actions, we can conquer sin by trusting Christ to change our affections."[6] — **David Platt**

C. S. Lewis wrote:
Indeed, if we consider the unblushing promises of reward and the staggering nature of the rewards promised in the Gospels, it would seem that our Lord finds our desires not too strong, but too weak. We are half-hearted creatures, fooling about with drink and sex and ambition when infinite joy is offered us, like an ignorant child who wants to go on making mud pies in a

slum because he cannot imagine what is meant by the offer of a holiday at the sea. We are far too easily pleased.[7]

"It's not that your desires are too *strong* and need to be dialed back; actually they're too *weak* and need to be redirected. ...The problem isn't *desire*. The problem is *misplaced* desire."[8] — **Tierce Green**

The common theme in these quotes is that our attempts to only fix our *behavior* will never transform us! We have to get down to the *root desires* and realize what's going on.

Idols take a good desire and twist it by promising that they can meet that desire better than God can!

They *cannot* deliver on that promise, yet we keep going with it because we've bought into their lies. This is the oldest temptation known to humans (**Gen 3.1-5**), and the core issue behind continued struggles with sin.

Our *Freedom Key*:
Strive to make your affection for God greater than your affection for sin!

This realization is an integral piece to the freedom solution so many Christians are missing!
So how do we put this into practice, in the midst of a stronghold that may seem overwhelming at times?

Authentic Manhood's "Battle Plan" tells us to
"Admit the Struggle, Identify the Lie, Replace with the truth."[9]
Kyle Idleman's recipe for AHA transformation tells us we need
"A Sudden Awakening, Brutal Honesty, and Immediate Action."[10]
What if we combined these?

Our *Freedom Plan* (5 Parts)

1) Recognize the stronghold!
What is the surface idol that I keep falling to? What is the deep idol behind it?

2) Name its empty promise!
Why is this idol appealing to me?
What is the lie? What is my misdirected desire, and the desire behind that?

3) Supersede that with God's truth!
"Supersede" implies that we're replacing that lie with something *better*.
Trust that pursuing your core desire *God's way* — will *always* be more *satisfying* and *rewarding* long term. (This flows from our *freedom key*.)
That means pursuing your relationship with God Himself more deeply. It means trusting Him that doing things His way —and not taking shortcuts— will be *worth* the reward!

4) Take immediate action!

Have I been procrastinating with my relationship with God? Take action!

Especially when we're *in a moment of temptation*, the truth won't matter if it pops into our head — but then we yield to the temptation anyway.

So when tempted, and the Spirit reminds you of the truth of what's *really* going on, take immediate action! Remove yourself from the tempting situation! Spend time with God right then! Seek accountability! Listen to the Spirit's lead and start to follow it, knowing you'll receive the *greater blessing!*

5) Reaffirm the truth until it sticks!

Strongholds are strongholds, not because we fell to the temptation the first time, but because we've worn a path there.

When we've internalized the lies and empty promises of an idol (maybe for years), it usually takes more than a single dose of truth to displace them! We need to keep repeating that truth to ourselves until we've internalized it more than the lie, and it becomes the louder voice.

So find Scripture passages and Christian quotes that will help *proclaim the truth* that deals with a particular stronghold. Print them and place them where you'll read them every day. Make flash cards. Copy a key verse or quote to your journal everyday. Memorize it!

We tend to be drawn to whatever we keep putting in front of ourselves.
So make that God and His Word, rather than tempting situations.

This step will help you wear a new path in your brain and heart. It will begin to replace the stronghold on a long-term basis, resulting in… **F R E E D O M !**

Let's come back to Paul's struggle with sin and his rescue story. He attributed his ongoing deliverance to both Jesus Christ and the Holy Spirit, but we didn't get to the *how* part of Paul's story.

Read Rom 8.14-16,28,34-39.

Paul talked about *listening to* and *following* the Spirit, approaching God as his *Daddy* ("Abba"), *trusting God* to work for his *good*, and *resting securely* in the *love* of Christ! So, just like we talked about, Paul strove to make his affection for God greater than his affection for sin! He kept God's goodness, His relationship, and His leading at the forefront of that battle against sin. And <u>that</u> is still the <u>Freedom Key</u> behind our Freedom Plan:

Strive to make your affection for God greater than your affection for sin!

From our earlier lessons, we know how to get started with this!

Maybe we've been gaining ground and developing a closer relationship with God.
Or maybe we need to refocus our attention on Him.
But God has given us everything we need to break those strongholds and experience His full freedom!

We need to draw near and trust Him!

 **Share Truth**

In his *Free Guide**, Brian Tome said, "God has freed us, in part, so we can put courage into others. As we do, we find that we experience more freedom, ourselves."[11]

How can we share the truth of this lesson with others? How do we pass this on?

For starters, we could...
☐ **share our Freedom Key and Freedom Plan**
   with someone who's wrestling with a stronghold in their life!

Better yet, as we *implement* that plan, we could...
☐ **share our personal rescue story!**

Best is probably doing both!

So as I start to experience freedom from something that has kept me in bondage, how can I best assemble my story to share with others? Here's a simple recipe from *Free Guide**[12] for...

☐ **sharing your freedom story:**

I used to believe:

Because I believed this, I used to:

These things made me feel:

The turning point came when:

Now I'm staying free by:

Moving forward, one way my life will be different is:

Pray

Pray that you'll each pursue and experience a deeper passion for Jesus.
Pray for freedom from bondage to idolatry.

1   *33 The Series. Volume 3 Training Guide: A Man and His Traps*, (Little Rock, AR; Authentic Manhood, 2013), 12-14.
2   *33 The Series. Volume 3 Training Guide: A Man and His Traps*, (Little Rock, AR; Authentic Manhood, 2013) 11.
3   *33 The Series. Volume 3 Training Guide: A Man and His Traps*, (Little Rock, AR; Authentic Manhood, 2013) 11.
4   Timothy Keller, *Galatians For You* (USA; The Good Book Company, 2013) 155.
5   Brian Tome, *Free Guide*: A companion guide to Brian Tome's Free Book* (Nashville; Thomas Nelson, 2010) 70.
6   David Platt, *Follow Me* (USA; Tyndale House Publishers, Inc., 2013) 111.
7   C.S. Lewis, *The Weight of Glory* (New York; Harper Collins, 1949) 26.
8   *33 The Series. Volume 3 Training Guide: A Man and His Traps*, (Little Rock, AR; Authentic Manhood, 2013) 44.
9   *33 The Series. Volume 3 Training Guide: A Man and His Traps*, (Little Rock, AR; Authentic Manhood, 2013) 45.
10 Kyle Idleman, *AHA: Awakening. Honesty. Action* (USA; David C Cook, 2014) 19.
11 Brian Tome, *Free Guide*: A companion guide to Brian Tome's Free Book*, (Nashville; Thomas Nelson, 2010) 73.
12 Brian Tome, *Free Guide**, 89.

Part IV: THE WALK

We've laid a foundation. We've looked past the physical. We've begun to build some momentum. In our final section, we'll begin to work on the walk that people will see lived out. These last three lessons cover just the tip of the iceberg. We will also begin to turn the corner as apprentices to prepare ourselves for continued growth in our walks *beyond* this curriculum.

10. Bushel [Purity & Sobriety]

Pray

Reflect

Has anything shifted in our strongholds or freedom story since we met last time?

Our goal from the beginning has been to make disciples who will disciple others.
If you've started your own discipleship group already, how is that going?

If not, have you considered that?
Is there anything specific that may be holding you back (other than a busy schedule)?
Do you need anything from us?

Is your relationship with God where you want it to be right now?
If not, why do you think that might be?
Should we adjust anything in regard to encouragement or accountability?

Media Placeholder: Bushel

An American *bushel* is a unit of dry measure equal to 8 gallons. A *bushel basket* is a thin, light wooden basket that holds a bushelful of produce or grain.

A bushel basket often represents *harvest*. Around Michigan, it's seen holding apples or other orchard fruits. It's a very handy tool for orchards and small farms.

Disciples of Jesus are meant to "bear fruit." Jesus wants us to bear fruit in our own lives. He also wants us to be harvesters (sharing the Gospel) in others' lives. So a bushel basket can be a great illustration for us — especially as we move into this fourth leg of our discipleship journey talking about our *walk* as Christians. To use a few biblical metaphors, our "walk" can also refer to "bearing fruit," or "being light."

The old children's song, *This Little Light of Mine*,[1] by Harry Dixon Loes, says, "This little light of mine, I'm gonna let it shine…" Verse 2 says, "Hide it under a bushel? No! I'm gonna let it shine…"

The song was inspired from:

Matt 5.14-16 (KJV) *"Ye are the light of the world. A city that is set on an hill cannot be hid.* [15] *Neither do men light a candle, and put it under a bushel, but on a candlestick; and it giveth light unto all that are in the house.* [16] *Let your light so shine before men, that they may see your good works, and glorify your Father which is in heaven.*

The King James Bible is where the songwriter got the idea of hiding your light under a "bushel." The ESV, NASB, and HCSB translate that word as "basket," and the NIV as "bowl." But according to the Mt 5.15 note from the *Treasury of Scripture Knowledge*,[2] the Greek word referred to "A measure containing about a pint less than a peck." (For those of us not well-versed in our volume units, that would be 1⅞ gallons.)

Jesus was referring to a container that held that standard measure of dry grain or flour. The point was to *not hide* our light, but *let it shine*.

An interesting side-effect of hiding your light under this basket is that, with your basket upside down, you wouldn't be able to collect any harvest. You could say that hiding our light makes us *fruitless*!

So we're going to start this final section by covering two topics that are very important to our witness and our ability to shine clearly. They are topics that would quickly cover our light and spill our fruit if we're not careful to pursue them. They are *purity* and *sobriety*.

[Purity & Sobriety]

 **Know Truth**

It might seem odd to combine these topics. Purity and sobriety are very different in numerous ways! Yet the thing they have in common is how quickly their opposites (sexual immorality and intoxication) can become idols in our lives and destroy our fruit and our witness. Purity and sobriety are also lifestyles that are highly opposed to the message that Hollywood and pop culture promote. So as we begin to talk about living out our Christian walks, these are key topics for us to lead with.

The Bible actually links our two topics together in the context of letting our light shine.

Read Rom 13.11-14.

Sexual impurity and drunkenness belong to the night. Sin loves the dark! But disciples are called to *be* light! God wants us to *wake up* from our slumber! He doesn't want us to be passive about the sin around us. He for sure doesn't want us to participate in it! He wants us to *put on* the armor of light (v12); He wants us to *put on* Jesus Himself (v14)! He wants us to behave like the *disciples* He's called us to be!

> **"Salvation is nearer?"**
> The book of Romans was addressed to "saints," i.e. *Christians* (**Rom 1.7**). So what did Paul mean when he wrote in **Rom 13.11** that, "our salvation is nearer than when we first believed" (HCSB)? Weren't his readers already saved? Yes they were!
> Earlier in Romans (**Rom 8.23**), Paul referred to the eager expectation of our *completed* adoption — that is, when God redeems our *bodies* and replaces them with our eternal, glorified bodies. When we were saved in this life, God redeemed our spirit. Yet we remain in these sin-loving bodies for now — *which explains the ongoing struggle!* So when he said we're closer to our salvation, he was referring to the complete fruition of it, when we'll get to live in God's presence forever, in bodies freed from sin. Hallelujah!

Gifts from God

Before we're tempted to make this all about rules, let's recognize that God *invented* both *sex* and *alcohol*. Not only that, but He *intended them* for our *pleasure!* They were His good design, and *neither* one is inherently evil.

Discuss what you observe about each of the following passages.
In particular, pay attention to the message being communicated about sex or alcohol. Is it viewed as evil or sinful? Or is it portrayed as something to enjoy with thankfulness? Is it something barely allowable but not really recommended? What do you see?

Read Ps 104.1,14-15; John 2.1-11; Gen 1.27-28; Song 7.6-9; 1Cor 7.3-5.

Boundaries from God

Though sex and alcohol are blessings from God, they are only blessings in *certain contexts*. In the *right* context, these two subjects can bring enjoyment and refreshment that can even *enhance* our fruitfulness in others areas of our lives!

But outside of those contexts, they cross the boundary into sin. Instead of a blessing, they bring guilt, shame, and <u>un</u>fruitfulness. When we feel guilty about sin, that will make us unfruitful. Our focus becomes about hiding our sin rather than bearing fruit for God. Outside the boundaries, we can lose our passion for pursuing God, because we become addicted to pursuing an idol.

If we're *in* that struggle, but don't correct our course, three things might happen. We'll *either* live in constant shame, *or* we'll put on the mask of the hypocrite and become "calloused" in our hearts (**Eph 4.19**), *or* we'll reject the authority of God's Word and pretend everything is okay. Yet if we can trust the Bible for our salvation, how could we not trust it for daily living?

So what are those healthy boundaries?

• The Law of the Land

Read Rom 13.1-2. (Titus 3.1 and **1Pet 2.13-14** give a similar instruction.)

God tells us to not only obey *Him*, but to obey our *government*. Of course, if the authorities ever give instructions that *contradict* God's instructions, we should choose obedience to God (as demonstrated in **Acts 4.18-20**).

So in the United States, that means if you're under the age of 21, it's illegal for you drink alcohol. (Communion would be the only exception — though most churches serve unfermented grape juice for that anyway.) And if it's *illegal* (and doesn't go against God's Word), that puts it outside our boundaries, and thus makes it <u>*sinful*</u>.

There are also occasions in America where sex is illegal (e.g. rape, sex with an unwed minor, etc), but those conditions are already considered sinful in the Bible. In general, our nation's laws and culture have a much looser view of sex than God's standard — but disciples of Jesus are called to God's *higher standard*.

• Biblical Boundaries for Sex and Alcohol

Assuming it's *legal* for someone to partake in alcohol…

**Drinking becomes sin as we approach <u>*drunkenness*</u>,
or as we <u>*impair our ability to think clearly and honor God*</u> in our decisions.**

Read 1Pet 1.13-16.

How important are clear thoughts for rejecting temptations and living out holy actions?

Regarding sex, our culture glamorizes pretty much any form of willing sex. But in God's eyes, and by His design, there is *one context* where sex is a *blessing* rather than a sin.

Sex is a blessing between a *man* and *woman* who are *married* to one another.
God counts it as sin in every other context.

We need to remember that sin is sin, not because it's an offense against culture,
but because it's an offense against *God* and *His* laws.

1Cor 6.9-11 (NASB) *Or do you not know that the unrighteous will not inherit the kingdom of God? Do not be deceived; neither <u>fornicators,</u> nor idolaters, nor <u>adulterers, nor effeminate, nor homosexuals,</u>* ¹⁰ *nor thieves, nor the covetous, nor <u>drunkards,</u> nor revilers, nor swindlers, will inherit the kingdom of God.* ¹¹ *Such <u>were</u> some of you; but you were washed, but you were <u>sanctified,</u> but you were justified in the name of the Lord Jesus Christ and in the Spirit of our God.*

First of all, note that the verb "*were*" in verse 11 gives us confidence that God is always more concerned with our present and future than our past!

This passage connects the topics of sexual impurity and drunkenness again, clearly listing them among sins that separate us from God.
    This particular *translation* makes some distinctions that might be overlooked in other translations. Where most modern English translations use the term "sexually immoral," the NASB uses the word "fornicators," which better conveys the idea of the Greek word πόρνοι (pornoi). The term "sexually immoral" might lead some to think, *Well, that's just referring to "immoral" sex* (based on cultural opinion rather than God's Word)— *as in really perverted practices, visiting prostitutes, or sleeping around with lots of people.*
    Yet a "fornicator" is simply anyone who has sex with someone they're not married to. (This would include someone you're not married to *yet*.)

The passage also makes God's expectation of gender roles clear.
This is not an issue of love versus hate — ***Christians are called to love everybody!***
It's not an issue of "judging" or looking down on people who are different from us.
It's simply an issue of *sanctification*. Will *I* <u>submit</u> to the will of my <u>Lord</u>?

Read Matt 5.27-28.

If we "only" take sex out of context in our *imagination*, does Jesus still count that as *sin*?

It's important to remember that having a *tempting thought* (or a *tendancy* toward certain thoughts) does *not* make us guilty of sin. Jesus Himself was *tempted*, yet did not sin (**Mt 4.1-11; Heb 4.15**).

Rather, it's when we *pursue* that thought rather than rejecting it or "taking it captive" that it crosses the line into sin.

Letting Your Light Shine _Clearly_

Read 1Cor 10.30-33; Rom 14.19-21.

Is it good to partake in God's gifts with thankfulness?

Should we take care that our freedom doesn't become a stumbling block for someone else?

Let's unpack the balancing point between those.

People jump to conclusions all the time! We can't stop that, and we shouldn't be uptight about that. Yet we should make sure our words and actions won't make it _easy_ for seekers or young Christians to jump to the _wrong conclusions_. Here are some examples:

If a certain person sees me with a beer or glass of wine, will they know the context that I'm _not_ continuing to excess? (The idea of stopping at 1 or 2 may be foreign to their experience.)

Or if I'm interacting with a mixed group of college students including those under 21, and I start talking about my favorite alcoholic drinks — if they don't have the context of God's boundaries, or know that I stay within those, what are they likely to conclude is acceptable for themselves?

What about the crude jokes I laugh at (or participate in)?
What about playing music that invites uses of sex or alcohol that are clearly outside of God's boundaries?

Or what if a boyfriend or girlfriend is over late at night, and my bedroom door is closed — or if they _spend the night_ in my bedroom? _Even if_ we are _not_ having sex together, we're _sending the message_ to the people around us that we probably _are_, or _will be_ once our will power runs low. (Remember, it's not about will power, but our affection for God — but that's the message we'd be sending.)

We _don't_ have to explain everything we do to every person. And we _do_ have _freedom_ to enjoy blessings from God within the proper contexts. We should just _take care_ to let our light shine _clearly_, and not send contradicting signals.

This will probably look different from different people, but the point is to be intentional.

A healthy byproduct of communicating to others that we have clear boundaries is that it keeps those boundaries clearer in our minds as well.

Further Study

There is much more that God's Word teaches about these topics. Here are additional passages that also list our two-fold topic together: **Gal 5.16-25**; **1Pet 4.1-7**; **Prov 23.26-35**; **Eph 5.3-18**; **1Cor 5.9-11**.

There are many more passages that cover the topics separately. Would it be interesting or helpful to study them more? Go for it! What other insights might you discover from your own study?

Process Truth

God designed sex and alcohol to be blessings in the right context. Some people grew up perceiving that sex and/or alcohol are always bad, dirty, or evil — that a Christian should never consume alcohol, or that sex is a necessary evil to propagate the human race. Others of us may have grown up in an environment where there were no limits other than perhaps "being safe." Or maybe your family gave no input whatsoever, and left you to come up with your own ideas about these topics.

What was your perception of sex and alcohol growing up?

Has that perception changed over time, whether through culture, opportunity, or Christian maturity?

Were any new concepts or perspectives introduced in the Know Truth section?

Think about how the areas of purity and sobriety affect your Light.
How would you rate your light *currently* (specifically with regard to these topics)?
• **Hidden under a bushel** (stronghold of idolatry)
• **Lampshade** (struggle with some oopses)
• **Smudged bulb** (not being careful to send clear signals to those around me)
• **On its stand** (presently demonstrating purity and sobriety)
• **Reflector and magnifying lens** (never ever struggled with these in action or thought) (Liar! ☺)

Read James 5.16 and 1John 1.5-9.

It's okay if anyone feels awkward talking about this. If there are currently any struggles going on, embarrassment could tempt us to keep that locked down and hidden. Pride could keep us from asking for help.
　　　But our goal is *healing*, *care*, and *continued growth* as disciples.

If it would be helpful for anyone to share more of their story,
this is a safe time and place to do that.

 **Apply Truth**

Freedom

When we've failed at purity or sobriety, Satan sees that as a perfect opportunity to keep us down and backed into a corner so that we halt our growth. But it's important to remember justification and sanctification again.

As Christians, we are already 100% forgiven (completely justified). Jesus paid for all of our past, present and future sins. God *considers* us as *worthy* because Jesus has overlaid *His worthiness* onto us. (That's the *start* of sanctification.) And over time, we keep making adjustments —with the Holy Spirit's help— to line up with God's will. (The *continued process* of sanctification.)

Confessing to *one another* allows us to move forward in that we no longer have to worry about *hiding* sin. Our prayers for one another can bind the enemy and bring encouragement and felt healing. They can help tune us to what the Holy Spirit is saying.

Confessing to *God* about specific sins doesn't affect our *forgiveness*, because we're already *completely* forgiven. But continuing in the practice of confessing sin to God *removes obstacles* to our relationship *closeness* with Him, to our *growth*, and to our *fruitfulness*.

Read Matt 15.18-20.

Just like we learned with idolatry in general, the **long term solution** to be delivered from any strongholds (or oopses) in these areas doesn't start with outward rules or behavior modification…

**It starts with accepting God's good design in our hearts and minds,
and waiting to enjoy that in the context of His blessing.**

That flows straight out of our **Freedom Key** from last week, which was to:
Strive to make our affection for God greater than our affection for sin!

And *from that attitude*… our long term solution is to keep applying our **Freedom Plan**:
1) **Recognize the stronghold.**
2) **Name its empty promise.**
3) **Supersede that with God's truth.**
4) **Take immediate action.**
5) **Reaffirm the truth until it sticks.**

Accountability

If anyone would like accountability in the area of purity or sobriety, ask for that now,
and talk through a specific plan that would be most helpful.
How should it be implemented?
Who would it be best to come through?

Letting our Lights Shine

Read 1Th 5.5-8 and 1Pet 2.9-12.

The goal of purity and sobriety is not to avoid sex and alcohol at all costs. It's *really* not even to avoid impurity and drunkenness. **The goal is embracing God's good design!** This will result in both our own blessing and allowing our lights to shine. Don't make it about *not doing* the bad, but about *desiring* God's best and allowing Him to use us for His glory.

 Share Truth

How do we share this with others?

The *best way* would be to **let our lights shine clearly** by *getting to*, or *staying in* a place of purity and sobriety in our walks.

☐ **We can give good counsel to fellow Christians** who are struggling in these areas or talking about it. Not making it about rules, but **about pursuing God's best** for their lives. We can **offer them accountability** — but make sure we share our **freedom key** and **freedom plan** to make it about increasing our desire for God and accepting His good plan.

☐ If we have a friend who we think is living in the right context, but their habits or words are sending a confusing message to young Christians or seekers, we can **speak into their life about setting a good example**.

Can you think of more ways to share this truth?

☐

☐

 **Pray**

Pray for healing, freedom, comfort, and deep acceptance of God's good plan.

---

1 Harry Dixon Loes, *This Little Light of Mine*, public domain.
2 Canne, Browne, Blayney, Scott, and others; introduction by R. A. Torrey, *Treasury of Scripture Knowledge* (circa 1880) public domain.

11. Mirror [Stewardship]

Pray

Reflect

How is your personal relationship with God?
How would you describe it right now?

Were there any clear *temptations* in the areas of purity or sobriety since we talked about those last time? If so, how did you respond to those situations or thoughts?

If there were any recent strongholds in your life (with these or other issues), **have you seen any movement in your strongholds since we received some training in how to break free from them?** (Progress? A step backwards because the enemy is really pushing back? The beginning of Freedom?)

If you haven't noticed yet, we keep coming back to sharing the Good News of Jesus Christ with others. Is the purpose of that to beat ourselves up if we haven't been pursuing opportunities for that? No! it's to encourage us *to pursue* those opportunities! The Gospel is often overlooked — even among many *church* cultures. Yet as true *disciples* of Jesus, we need to keep setting that in front of us to remind us that this is our *main purpose* as members of the Church — to make disciples: baptizing them and teaching them to obey. All Christians are not gifted as evangelists, yet all are called to *do what they can* to expand God's Kingdom.
How are you doing with finding opportunities to lead into the Gospel?

Media Placeholder: Mirror

A mirror is an object that reflects. The earliest mirrors were simply reflecting pools, which reflected a dim image that was easily distorted by a slight wind or a little vibration. Mirrors were developed more over the centuries, but for a long time they were still not ideal, since they were either warped, tinted, or easily scratched. But the modern metal-backed, flat glass mirror reflects a very clear, accurate image. It reflects what *is*.

A rearview mirror on a car reflects where you've been. You can glance at that to see what has passed. In a way, a rearview mirror reflects what *was*.

Mirrors reflect our *surroundings* very well — whether what *is* around us, or what *was* recently around us if we're on the move. Either way, they reflect the *outside*.

But what if there was a way to reflect the *inside* — either where we are, or where we've recently been?

Prov 27.19 (NIV) *As water reflects the face, so one's life reflects the heart.*

There are actually a couple of ways we could witness that internal reflection. Maybe not a *perfect* reflection, yet still quite revealing. One of those ways would be to take a look at someone's *calendar* and see how they use their *time*. Of course that depends on how much they fill a calendar out, or what kinds of things they include on their calendar. But if there were some calendar we could look at that detailed how someone used every waking minute — it would reveal a lot about their heart.

Another way to see a reflection of someone's heart would be to take a look at their *checkbook register*. What if someone were to study *your* checkbook register? Or your bank statement? Or credit card statement? However you keep track of your finances, what if someone could see *each transaction* and what it was used for? Would it reveal what we'd *want* it to reveal?

Luke 12.34 (ESV) [Jesus said,] *For where your treasure is, there will your heart be also.*

Do our *finances* reflect where our *hearts* have been? Or do our *hearts* reflect where we've put our *finances*? Whichever is the cause or effect, they are connected. And a *disciple* will try to direct *both* toward God's glory.

[Stewardship]

Know Truth

Why do Christians often use the word "stewardship" when they talk about finances?

Stewardship conveys the idea of being a *steward* — someone who *looks after* or *manages* something (or someone) on behalf of another. A flight attendant — which used to be called a *steward* or *stewardess* — looks after passengers on behalf of an airline. Business stewards look after the money and investments of their employer.

Likewise when Christians apply the word *stewardship* to our finances, it can remind us that we're managing *God's belongings* which *He's entrusted* to us. Listen to God's words in the following Psalm.

Psalm 50.9-12 (NIV) *I have no need of a bull from your stall*
or of goats from your pens,
10 *for every animal of the forest is mine,*
and the cattle on a thousand hills.
11 *I know every bird in the mountains,*
and the insects in the fields are mine.
12 *If I were hungry I would not tell you,*
for the world is mine, and all that is in it.

All of the physical creation *belongs to* God.

Read Gen 2.15; Gen 1.27-28.

Adam's very first instruction from God —even before Eve was created— was to *take care* of the Garden of Eden. Then after God created Eve, their first instructions together were to be fruitful, and to *rule over* all the other creatures. So from the beginning, God created mankind to be *stewards*.

This idea of stewardship doesn't *only* apply to gardens and animals, but also to our environment, our businesses, our ministries, our relationships, our bodies, our time, and yes, even our money. Stewardship applies to anything and everything in this life that God entrusts to our care.

So *who we are* on the inside is going to play out in how we steward our "possessions."

Prov 10.16 (ESV) *The wage of the righteous leads to life, the gain of the wicked to sin.*

If my heart is righteous (because I'm working with God on being sanctified), my income is ultimately going to go toward *life-giving* things. Things like taking good care of my body and spirit, providing for my family, investing in relationships, or giving to God's work.

But if my heart is wicked, I'll direct my income toward *life-draining* things such as selfishness, unhealthy balances, messages *opposed* to God, and even sin itself.

Let's link **Prov 10.16** back to our mirror illustration.

The outcome of my income is a reflection of my heart.

In the following passages, what additional insights can you draw between our hearts and our money? **Mark 7.21-23**; **2Cor 9.6-8**; **Matt 6.19-21,24**; and **1Tim 6.6-10**.

Now don't freak out — but we're going to mess up our traditional lesson order here. ☺ We'll discuss the **Apply Truth** section *next*, then come back and **Process** that.

Apply Truth

The Bible addresses stewardship more than any other single topic — including faith, prayer, forgiveness, holiness, and love! Why?

God did that because He knew it would be a *huge obstacle* for so many people throughout all generations! He also chose stewardship to be an avenue for *great blessing!* And it's an integral part of everyday life.

So God's Word contains a "wealth" of info about finances. It would be easy to beat this topic to death with an information overload. But instead, we're going to boil it down to a few practical principles.

Long Term Experiment
Just to open our eyes to the magnitude of what the Bible says about this topic, here's a little challenge. As you keep working on getting God's Word in you, choose a special highlight color that you haven't used before in your Bible or Bible app. Whenever you read a verse or passage that talks about money, possessions, wealth, etc, highlight it in that special color! (Use *other* colors to highlight different aspects of God's Word. You might end up building your own color code system — or not. But try this one out!)

---

4 Basic Principles of Godly Stewardship

If we apply these to our lives, they will have a *profound* effect on our future. But even though these principles are very simple and straightforward, they are seldom applied all together in our society. And therefore few people experience the *blessings* that go along with them.

1) Practice Diligence

This could be considered Step "0." It's really a lead-in for finances. This one directly affects our *income*, while the other 3 principles apply to the "*outcome* of our income" (where we put our money).

Diligence is hard work, but it's more than that. It's *careful* work. *Dedicated* work. So it's a reflection of my heart just as much as the principles about *using* my money.

Read Prov 10.4; Prov 28.19; Prov 6.9-11.

What do these proverbs tell us about how diligence will affect our income?

Read the parable in Matt 25.14-30.

How did the master respond to the work ethic of the first two servants?

How did the master respond to the work ethic of the third servant?

Read Col 3.22-24.

According to this passage, where should we find our motivation for practicing diligence?

2) Avoid Debt

This concept has become pretty strange to our culture. Car dealerships rarely even tell you the cost of a vehicle anymore — only its monthly payment. Yet debt can steal your future freedom!

Read Prov 22.7 and Matt 18.23-25.

In Bible times, there was no such thing as bankruptcy. If you racked up a debt that you could not pay, the legal consequence was that you were sold into slavery until you paid off your debt. So the borrower was *literally* slave to the lender.

Today that's not the case. Yet **debt comes at the expense of our future *financial* freedom.** By purchasing something we cannot afford, it's like *stealing money* from our own future! Debt is an easy way to put ourselves in bondage to stuff.

The trap of debt is the interest that's charged! With interest, you have to *pay back <u>more than</u> what you received!* And the longer it takes to pay that off, the *amount you end up paying* goes up exponentially!

Here's an example of real math for credit card debt. Let's say you racked up $5,000 of credit card debt. And let's say your *interest rate* —after your "low introductory rate" expires— settles in at 20.99%. (A pretty realistic number — read the fine print.) If you never racked up more than that initial $5,000 of debt, and sent in $300/month toward paying it off, it would take 1 year and 9 months to pay it off, and would cost you a total of $6,000 ($1,000 *more than* the *value* of what you purchased)!

On the other hand, if you only put $100/month toward that initial $5,000 of debt, at the same interest rate, it would take you *10 years* to pay it off! And it would cost a total of *$12,000!* That's like buying your stuff for 240% of its value! What a deal! 😬

It's all about the math, not how convincing a salesperson or ad campaign is!

There are simple, free online debt calculators that will do the math for you. If you enter what you can afford to pay, they can calculate how long it would take to pay the debt off. Or if you want to get it paid off by a certain deadline, they can calculate what monthly payment that would require. It's all about the math!

Sometimes the math works out in your favor. For example, if you find a *really low* interest rate for a car loan, and can pay it off *really quickly*, the interest you end up paying may only be a *couple hundred* dollars. That might seem like a small "convenience fee" for getting that vehicle now.

Or — getting that new vehicle might make you pay through the nose for years, and end up paying *thousands more* than the car was initially worth. But you have to use a loan calculator and *do the math* to know which it is.

Or a $100,000 school loan might make sense if that will help you get a six-figure salary. That would be a wise financial investment. But racking up a $100,000 school debt to be a retail cashier is basically submitting yourself to a lifetime of financial slavery. It's all about the math!

Read Rom 13.7-8.

God's Word teaches Christians to pay what they owe, and that it's best to not be in debt at all! (Except the continuing debt to love one another!)

> **Debt of love**
> Does that mean we're supposed to "keep track"? As in, they did something nice for me, and now I'm obligated to do something nice for them? No. Love is supposed to be full of grace. But if we treated people *as if* we always owe them love (whether or not they've done anything for us), that's just a good way to always maintain a loving attitude.

Does that mean it's bad to *ever* use debt?
If you are borrowing *now* for a good chance of a higher return *later* — that's very a wise and God-honoring way to steward your money. Things like school loans, business investments, and mortgages would fall into this category — but only when the math works out!

What about credit cards?
If I do not have the discipline to pay off a credit card every month, it's *unwise* for me to be using one! Carrying a balance from month to month actually *hurts* our credit. It points us in the direction of financial slavery, and tunes our hearts to *instant gratification* and *selfishness* rather than *godly patience* and *reliance* on Him.

But if I get a rewards credit card with no annual fee, and I pay off the full balance every month, that is *very wise*. It <u>builds</u> my credit, and the rewards actually generate a little *income* over time. We pay no interest if we pay off credit cards every month. Establishing credit like this can help us make future investments, such as purchasing a home and building wealth through equity, as opposed to paying rent forever.

The question of debt is all about the math! Would it *help* my future ability to honor God with my finances? Or would it *hurt* my future ability to honor God with my finances?

3) Be Generous

Avoiding debt is all about the *math*. But being generous is *not* about the math; it's about God's *blessing*. Consider this Proverb…

Prov 11.24 (ESV) *One gives freely, yet grows all the richer;*
another withholds what he should give, and only suffers want.

If generosity were only a matter of adding and subtracting, we'd think the person who retained more for himself would be the "richer" one. But that's not the case in God's economy. So the difference isn't math. The difference is that God <u>blesses</u> generosity!

That's not a financial promise. If I give $100, that doesn't guarantee that I'll receive $100 back. It's not a financial promise; it's a *spiritual* promise. So the blessing or riches we receive from being generous *may* be financial, but they may be relational, spiritual, physical, etc. The point is that God blesses generosity.

Read Mal 3.8-10. (Malachi is the book just before Matthew.)

In this passage… **What was the condition of receiving God's blessing?**

What was the condition of receiving His curse?

What specific test did God challenge them to?

> **With God's blessing, things work out better than they should, in our favor.**
> **With God's curse, things work out worse than they should, against us.**

The tithe — what is it?
A tithe means 10% of your total *gross* income.
In **Mt 22.21; Mk 12.17; Lk 20.25**, Jesus told us to "give to Caesar what is Caesar's, and to God what is God's." He did not say give to God from the leftovers after you've paid Caesar (which would be our *net* income).

The tithe was part of Old Testament Jewish law. Does the New Testament command Christians to tithe? (Remember the New Testament is God's law for Christians.)

- In **Mt 23.23** and **Lk 11.42**, Jesus condemned the Pharisees for being careful to tithe even from their herb gardens, while neglecting more important things like love and justice.

- In **Lk 18.12**, Jesus told a parable about a Pharisee who bragged about tithing.

- **Heb 7** talks about an Old Testament situation where Abraham gave a tithe to Melchizedek. (And the passage was really about the eternal authority of Christ.)

That's *all* the verses in the New Testament about tithing.
So actually, no, the New Testament does *not command* Christians to tithe.
But it *does* command us to be *generous!* (And that's conveyed in *many* passages!)

So if a tithe is what you were <u>expected</u> to give in the Old Testament (blessed if you do; cursed if you don't), and then the New Testament tells us to be <u>generous</u>… (Generous means giving *more* that what's expected, right?) — doesn't that make a compelling case for Christian generosity to *start at 10%* and go up from there? Again, that's not the Law, but *why wouldn't we* start at a tithe if we want God's blessing?

So *where* are Christians supposed to be generous? The Elk's Club? Saving the whales? Political campaigns? Their university alma mater? Cancer research? There is no end of destinations that people donate money toward. But God calls us to be generous specifically toward His work of *Christian ministry*.

<u>**The New Testament gives 3 examples of where Christians should give:**</u>

- **To their local church.** (As in **Acts 4.36-37; 1Tim 5.17-18.**)

- **To support missions to other places.** (As in **Php 4.10-19; Lk 8.1-3.**)
  This would include any ministry or missionary who helps spread the Gospel or serves in a place you're not — whether that's overseas or domestic.

- **To the needy (especially fellow Christians).** (As in **Mt 6.2-3; Rom 12.13; Rom 15.26.**)
  This shows the love of Christ by meeting physical needs.

4) Save

Read Prov 13.11,22.

Does God seem to be in favor of "get rich quick" schemes?

If I'm trying to take the "easy" route toward wealth, does that in general demonstrate diligence?

Does God seem to be in favor of *building wealth* over time (assuming I'm being generous along the way)?

What is the description of the person who can leave an inheritance for their grandkids?

Some Christians feel guilty about building wealth. But that's not God's intention. Consider this… If I *don't* build wealth over time, as I get older, I'm going to become one of those *needy* people that others will have to take care of. Then I won't have the *means* to be *generous* to anyone else. And what if I leave my family with nothing but debt or expenses?

In the Parable of the Talents, which we read earlier, the master left money with his servants for them to invest over time. In **Mt 25.27**, the master told the lazy servant that basically at the minimum, he should have left it with the bankers to build some interest. Interest is our enemy when it's working against us, but a *great ally* when it's working for us! As we save over time, the *least we could do* is put that money in an interest-bearing savings account. (Hint: credit unions tend to have higher savings interest rates than banks. You can compare online banking options too.) But you can bet the two guys in the parable who doubled their master's money invested a bit more aggressively than just putting it in a savings account! As we develop a regular income and can start putting money away, we can look into financial planners and investors, who can steward our money for long-term growth. Just make sure we're not bypassing generosity in order to hoard wealth!

 **Process Truth**

The outcome of my income is a reflection of my heart.

If someone were to take a look in that rearview mirror and see how you've *been* spending your finances —if they could see every dollar spent— would there be much evidence that you've invested in life-giving things?

Were these 4 stewardship principles mostly review for you, or was there anything eye-opening about them?

Have you been a regular tither (giving 10+% of your gross income toward God's work)?

If not, discuss if some of the passages we've looked at have been inspiring you to test God in His promise of blessing?

Do you think your relationship with debt up until now has been directing you toward future financial slavery?
(If so, Dave Ramsey's *Financial Peace*[1] or other resources could be a big help to you.)

Which of the 4 principles has been the hardest for you to apply? Why do you think that is?

Share Truth

☐ **Showing a little self-restraint/frugality with purchases around friends** could be a great example. (E.g. If money is tight, don't get the $10 fast food meal, when you could get by with the $3-$4 meal.)

☐ **Demonstrating generosity** is also a great way to pass these principles along!

What other ways might we bring these principles to people outside our discipleship group?

☐

☐

Pray

---

1 Dave Ramsey, *Financial Peace University Membership Kit* (USA; Financial Peace University, 2012).

12. Workwear [Service]

Pray

Start with each member of the group praying. Pray about the time we've spent together, continuing opportunities, and this final lesson.

Reflect

After today, we'll have covered twelve discipleship topics. There's no doubt that we *could've covered* three times that number without running short on important discipleship ideas. But these twelve were prayerfully chosen to give a very practical foundation for discipleship to prepare us for *personal* and *outward* application. **The goal was to get us to *learn how to think* through being Jesus' apprentice, so we'll be able to *carry that beyond this curriculum*.**

Here's a review of the topics we've covered so far (and their illustrations):
1.   **The Bible** (Telescope & Microscope)
2.   **The Gospel** (Life Preserver Ring)
3.   **Pursuing Vital Relationships** (Empty Bench)
4.   **Prayer & Fasting** (Sync Cable)
5.   **Stillness** (Spiritual Lemonade)
6.   **Spiritual Warfare** (Super Soldier)
7.   **Spirit-Led, Self-Responsible, Team-Supported** (Huddle)
8.   **Integrity** (Masks)
9.   **Removing Idols** (Shackles)
10.   **Purity & Sobriety** (Bushel)
11.   **Stewardship** (Mirror)

We have one more topic together as a group that we'll get to shortly.

Thinking through these lessons, our accountability, our relationships as a group, etc — what has been the most impactful for you, and why?

Of the topics we've covered, which area currently needs the most attention? What would be a good plan of action for that? (Write it out.)

Media Placeholder: Workwear

The boots and gloves pictured here send a clear message of purpose. We know them as "*work* boots" and "*work* gloves" — even if the place *we're* employed has no need for such workwear. But there's no doubt, these boots and gloves represent work in the form of physical labor. They're the kind of boots and gloves someone might wear in construction, in cultivating, or in demolition.

If we think of those three workwear uses *spiritually*, two of the three are *beneficial* to God's kingdom. Some people work to *build* or *grow* God's kingdom, while others work to tear it down. Those who tear down may do that *actively* (through things like gossip, judgment, or disobedience) or *passively* (through standing by idly and letting it fall into disrepair).

Prov 14.1 (NIV) *The wise woman builds her house,*
but with her own hands the foolish one tears hers down.

Now it would be pretty ridiculous to see a woman put on work gloves and safety glasses, grab a sledge hammer and crowbar, and physically begin to tear down her own house. That's *so foolish* that it's pretty much unthinkable. So it makes sense that the straightforward understanding of this proverb is as a *metaphor*.

The *wise* will do things to build up their *household:* showing love, being encouraging, spending time together, demonstrating self-control and patience, etc.

Whereas the *foolish* do things that rip apart their household: cruel words, hot temper, lack of patience or self-control, etc. It's not that anyone ever set out to ruin their family. But the foolish don't think through their attitudes or actions to *remove* the works that demolish and *add* works that build or grow.

How much more does this metaphor speak to *God's house*? (Not the Temple or the church building, but His household, His family!) Wise disciples will intentionally do what they can to build the church. Foolish (immature) Christians let their emotions and opinions tear down churches and church leaders. Or through inaction, they let that house slowly deteriorate.

This should *not* sound like a great burden for us disciples. No one is asking us to singlehandedly perform some work or service that will turn around the American church. Rather, wise disciples understand that we have some sort of active role to play in doing *what we can* —that is, doing *what God equips us for*— to serve the church or ministry He's placed us in. It might not be physical labor, it might not be on a stage, but God has a way for each of us to serve joyfully in a way that blesses others!

[Service]

 **Know Truth**

We learned in Lesson 7 (Huddle), that as members of the Church (and a particular church or ministry), we have a responsibility to serve our Coach and team.

In Lesson 8 (Masks), we started with the idea that God created humans in His image, and then that image was tarnished when sin entered the world. But then through accepting the Gospel, we are *re-created in His image* — as the Spirit begins to sanctify our character to line us back up with Jesus.

Did you realize these concepts are tied together?

Read Mk 10.45; Eph 2.8-10.

Jesus came to serve — and as new creations in Christ, He designed us *for good works*. That's a big part of being *sanctified* back to His image. So it's not just a *"responsibility"* to serve — but as we implement that, we gain the *satisfaction* of fulfilling our *purpose!* In this, it becomes a *joy* to serve, not just a duty.

> **As Christians, we are re-created in the image of Christ _for the purpose of serving!_**
> **And our service should in some way support the _mission of making disciples!_**

As we learn about this topic of service, we're also going to turn the corner in _how_ *we learn* about it. We're going to use a lot more questions to *help us draw the truth* from the passages ourselves. Besides helping us learn today's topic, this will set us up to *continue to* know, process, apply, and share God's truth for other topics *beyond* this curriculum.

Read 1Pet 4.10-11.

What do you observe about the passage?

Who does it tell us to serve?

Where should our confidence rest as we approach serving?

What two specific examples of giftedness does the passage give?

Read Rom 12.4-8.

What do you observe about this passage?

What specific examples of giftedness do you see listed?

Read 1Cor 12.4-12,27-31;14.12.

What do you observe here?

What specific examples of giftedness do you see listed in 1Cor 12.8-10?

What specific examples are listed in v28?

In v31, we're told to earnestly desire the "greater" or "higher" gifts. 1Cor 14.12 clues us in on those by encouraging us to excel in these. **What kind of gifts are those?**

Read Eph 4.11-13,16.

What do you observe?

Are the church leaders intended to do all the work of ministry? If not, who is supposed to help in that?

What happens to the church (the body of Christ) when all its members are functioning properly?

How does serving affect our Christian maturity?

So how do we begin to really know God's truth about _future topics_?
Beyond just reading a passage, we **make observations about what the text is actually saying**.
Who is it talking to?
Does the immediate context reveal details?
Do other passages about the same topic give added perspective?

Sometimes our observations will confirm what we believed. Sometimes they will teach us something new. Sometimes they will reveal flaws in what we previously thought.
As disciples, we should seek to keep _adjusting to_ God's Word.

Then beyond just _understanding_ what the truth is saying, we should _process_ that truth.

 Process Truth

1Pet 4.10-11 employed the word "serve" in both a general way and a specific way. The general way was referring to using _whatever giftedness we have_ to serve God and bless the church. The specific way was referring to having the spiritual gift of service (i.e. physical help, service projects, etc).

Do you think physical service is one of your stronger spiritual gifts?
If so, was that a new spiritual gift after becoming a Christian, or did you have a natural wiring for service even before you became a Christian?
(Sometimes our spiritual gifts are abilities we never had before, and sometimes they're _enhancements_ of natural gifts that God supercharges for serving the church.)

If physical service is not one of your strong suits, that's okay. We just need to be intentional about serving the Church in ways that use other forms of giftedness. And by the way, that doesn't let us off the hook from ever providing physical helps! Just like not being gifted in evangelism doesn't mean we should never seek to share the Gospel!

We saw earlier that God re-creates us in Christ for the _purpose_ of serving _Him_.
Do you find yourself "volunteering" your time or energy to causes that are void of God, church, or outreach intentions?

If so, do those efforts take time and energy away from ways you _could be_ serving Him through the church or outreach?

Have you _implemented_ any of your abilities in serving the church yet?
If so, what kinds of things have you helped with?

If there were any areas you were particularly *effective* at and *enjoyed*, those might point to a specific area of spiritual giftedness. **If so, what do you think those gifts may be?**

How do I know where God might want me to serve?
Has He shown you that He's starting to move —or wants to move— in a particular area? Has He put that on your heart? Does it keep popping up?

If so, *join God* in the work He's doing!

If you have *not* started serving the church yet, what areas might you want to try?

When would you implement that?

Would you need anything from current ministry leaders to help you get started? (Instructions, courage, etc. If so, communicate that! 😃)

Going beyond this lesson, **when we process the truth of Scripture, we take it to heart.**
We can ask, "Why does this matter?"
or "How does it affect or involve me?"
We let the truth convict us or challenge us or resonate with us.
The next step is to *apply* it.

Apply Truth

Once we've begun serving the church (or at least decided to), there are a few key aspects of implementation that will really help us in that goal of *growth* for the church (and ourselves). Regardless of our giftedness, those practical applications are **following through, serving wholeheartedly**, and **discipling others**.

Following Through

Read 2Cor 8.10-12.

This passage is in the specific context of serving through generosity. Paul strongly urged the Corinthians to follow through on a financial pledge they had made. They weren't expected to do something they weren't equipped for — only to finish what they talked about.

He wanted them to bring the *same intensity* to their *follow-through* as they had expressed in their *initial eagerness*.

Do you think this exhortation is fully transferable to other areas of giftedness and ministry?

Read Matt 21.28-31.

One son originally said *no*, but then had a change of heart and showed up to serve.
The other son said *yes*, then didn't follow through.

Is it the people who merely express willingness, or the people who show up and serve, who help the church function properly and grow?

In these passages, what emotions might you feel if you were in Paul's shoes with regard to the Corinthians, or in the father's shoes with regard to the second son?

Does that add perspective to the value of our own follow through and how it affects our leaders? If so, in what way?

Some people express willingness, but then don't follow through. Others initially resist, but then end up helping. **What's a third option that would be the biggest blessing to the church and its leaders?**

Serving Wholeheartedly

Read Php 2.13-15.

Have you ever worked with someone who grumbled in their job or service?

If so, what effect does that attitude have on the team atmosphere or the productivity of the work?

Read Col 3.17,23.

Whether we're helping a pastor, a ministry team leader, a church, a friend, the needy, etc, who should we consider ourselves to be *really* serving?

What level of effort does God expect from our service?

As imperfect disciples, there may have been times when we've dropped the ball in serving the church — whether serving half-heartedly or not following through. Maybe we didn't give it the attention to quality, preparation, or detail that we *would've* given it, had it been for a class or job. Maybe we forgot, or got distracted from it. It happens.

But when we *realize* we're guilty of this, we can be *tempted* to *avoid embarrassment* or *rebuke* by either not dealing with it (ignoring or hiding the fact that we dropped the ball), or just quietly slipping away into some hole. But remember how our enemy will do whatever they can to prevent Christians from glorifying God? That's where those temptations come from!

And remember how we have a responsibility as members of the church team? That means *accepting responsibility* for our failures as much as *taking responsibility* for doing our part.

So <u>what would be the *right way* to make a course correction?</u>

- **Remember God's grace!**

- **Face the situation.** Don't ignore it. Approach the ministry leaders about it.

- **Communicate about the dropped ball.** This might involve confessing, apologizing, and expressing a desire for another opportunity to serve.

- **Communicate about a plan.** Work on it together. Should you try again in the *same* area? Or should you try serving in a *different* area that better fits your giftedness or passions? Will you need training or encouragement to help you get started?

If we were to handle our failures like this, what would be the effect on our personal growth?

What would be the effect on the ministry we serve in?

Discipling Others

Besides discipling others with general Christian discipleship (like we've been learning through this entire curriculum), we can also disciple others in the specific ways we've learned to serve the church. We can find apprentices! This is valuable in both *multiplying* our effectiveness, and *replacing* ourselves.

Some ministry roles could be greatly enhanced if there were a bigger team helping with those. We can share our passion, interest, or reasons for serving the way we do. We can recruit others who may have the right giftedness, and show them what we do. Better yet, we could go beyond that and show them *what we'd like to do* if we had more time. That's when multiplying can start taking place!

Other ministry roles don't really need more than one person doing them — given the current size or circumstances of the ministry. Yet if you're the only person who fills that role, what happens when you're sick? What happens if you need a vacation? What if God gives you a desire to start serving in a *different* way? What happens if you were suddenly in a car accident, or needed to move away because of a job?

Would mass chaos ensue because no one else was equipped or encouraged to serve in the way you served? Would that aspect of ministry just not happen for a while? Would the responsibility fall back on the pastor? Would the leader be left scrambling to recruit an on-the-spot volunteer?

It's *healthy* for the long-term growth of the ministry —and our own discipling skills— if we equip others to come alongside us in the ways we serve.

Read Num 11.28; Ex 33.11; Num 27.18-21; and Dt 34.9.

Moses had a well-prepared replacement. The transition wasn't just a brief hand off and well-wish at the very end. Joshua apprenticed under Moses for a long time. He learned from Moses. He even lingered in God's presence at times for longer than Moses did.
     So when Moses died, the Israelites still had a strong leader!

But when Joshua died, **Judges 2.8-11** tells us that the very next generation started following idols. That's because Joshua *didn't replace himself*.

In a community church setting, there may be people excited to serve in a specific role for a very long time. Yet things can unexpectedly happen, so it's still good to be prepared.
     In a setting like campus ministry, the idea of replacing yourself would be much more urgent because people graduate every year.

So if you sense that your season of serving in a particular role may be coming to a close —maybe because you're moving away, or you desire to try serving in a new way— then it becomes even more urgent to recruit and train an apprentice. It's helpful to keep staff or core leaders in the loop about who you're thinking about apprenticing. They may be able to add valuable insights to help you select and train the next person. But as the person already in that role, it's helpful for you to be the one watching for that potential apprentice.

For topics beyond this curriculum, we can apply truth effectively when we **search for instructions or examples from the scripture, think through practical steps, and take action.**
     The sooner we take action the better. Otherwise we may lose our motivation for applying it.

Share Truth

What do you think? How do we communicate this to others?
How could I bring others alongside me with this topic?
(Consider personal example, social media, personal conversations, etc, as resources.)

- [ ]
- [ ]
- [ ]

The same question is helpful as we study future topics after this group. **Sharing Truth starts by asking the question, how could I bring others alongside me with this topic?**

Please see the following section, **Appendix A: What's Next**, for some ideas and instructions about continuing your discipleship journey after this study.

**Pray**

Appendices

Further resources for your discipleship journey.

A: What's Next?

A great way to *continue as a disciple who disciples* (if you haven't started this already) would be to find another Jesus follower or two and start your own discipleship group. Or, put renewed effort in considering who God would want you to share the Gospel with, and work toward that opportunity.

It's also important to keep growing in other topics as well. Here's a **starter list of topics** you may desire to know, process, apply, and share truth about — whether through personal study, a LifeGroup, etc.

How would I approach this if I didn't have a guide? Choose a Bible search engine, and search for keywords and their synonyms. Leave flexibility for different forms of the word, such as single or plural nouns or different verb tenses. Then sort through your results. When you find the passages that speak to your topic, follow our process:

Know Truth:	*Make observations about what the text is actually saying.*
Process Truth:	*Ask questions to take it to heart.*
Apply Truth:	*Search for instructions or examples, think through practical steps, take action.*
Share Truth:	*Consider how to bring others alongside you with this topic.*

Starter List of More Discipleship Topics

Active Listening
Flexibility
Being Attentive
Gratitude/Appreciation
Wisdom
Power of the Tongue
Boundaries
Patience
Hospitality
Risk/Courage
Fellowship
Time Management

Teachability
Selfishness
Honesty
Dependability
Respect/Honor
Margin/Space
Emotional Health
Contentment
Transparency
Worship
Assertiveness/Initiative
Forgiveness

Receiving Feedback
Humility
Friendliness
Unity
Compassion
Joy
Trials/Perseverance
Grace
Learning from Life
Leadership
Wisdom
Peace

B. All-in [Christian Baptism]

This extra resource can be studied as an individual or as a group. It can also be shared with others who are willing to learn about baptism.

Reflect

We should use extra care when approaching this topic. If we didn't know much about baptism coming into this study, it'll be relatively easy to assume an attitude of learning. But if we were "set" in our views of about it —and then if the Bible starts to *challenge* what we thought— we'll come to a crisis point: Will I *react to* that by pushing back in some way? Or will I *respond to* it by adjusting my beliefs, practice, and communication to line up with God's Word?

If you *do* find yourself at that crisis point, you can know that this study is the *result of* that adjusting process too! So you'd be in good company! 😉

There's *much* that the Bible teaches about Christian baptism — about 20 separate passages! In the context of this guide, this study is *not* meant to be exhaustive, or to address every alternative idea. But —as with the other lessons— it's intended to provide *enough* to get started on the right foot as becoming a disciple who disciples.

Reflect on your starting point with baptism for a moment.
Do you consider yourself very tied down to a current view of baptism?

If so, that's okay. But consider putting this study on hold *until* you'd be willing to adjust to God's Word — whatever it reveals.

Pray

Pray for openness and understanding (as is good with all biblical topics).
Ask God to help us let go of any presumptions we may have come to the table with.
Ask Him to speak clearly so we can know, process, apply, and share the truth He reveals through His Word.

Media Placeholder: All-In

Some Christians view gambling as a *big no-no* sin. But the Bible doesn't actually *condemn* gambling — it just *promotes* financial wisdom! *Every game* at the casino has a mathematical probability of winning that's *less than* 50%! That means if you play long enough, you *will lose money* overall! So if the odds are in favor of you *losing* money, that's not really financial wisdom!

Yet we're *not* supposed to always play it safe! God wants us to *take risks for Him!* Jesus told a couple of parables (**Mt 25.14-30** & **Lk 19.12-27**) where some servants invested their master's money. Some of the servants increased the initial investment twofold, fivefold, or even tenfold! You can *bet* those servants took some *investment risks* and didn't just put the money in the bank!

The parables also described *other servants* who didn't invest *anything*. They *thought* they were taking zero risk, but they ended up *losing everything* by failing to obey their master! Jesus told both parables in the context of the kingdom of heaven. Here are two more one-liner parables that Jesus told about the kingdom of heaven…

Matt 13.44-45 (ESV) *"The kingdom of heaven is like treasure hidden in a field, which a man found and covered up. Then in his joy he goes and <u>sells all that he has</u> and buys that field.*
⁴⁵ "Again, the kingdom of heaven is like a merchant in search of fine pearls, ⁴⁶ who, on finding one pearl of great value, went and <u>sold all that he had</u> and bought it.

There's a term in poker when a player goes *"all-in."* It means that player is *fully invested!* They put *all* their remaining chips in the pot. If they win, they win big; if they lose, they lose everything! The first servants in the parables from Matt 25 and Luke 19 were not "gambling" *per se*; they were "investing." But either way, the were risking big! They were *all-in!*

The other servants thought they were playing it safe. They kept the master at a "safe" distance. By not being *all-in*, they ended up not being *in* at all. By being passive about what the master told them to do, not only did they miss out on the blessing, but they received condemnation instead!

The same holds true with following Jesus. We either "risk" everything to be *all-in*, or we risk everything by *not being in* at all. There is no "kind of" being a Christian. The Bible gives us a clear way to publicly express our all-in commitment to Jesus. That expression is Christian baptism. That doesn't mean we'll be perfect after that; sanctification (becoming more holy) is a lifelong process! And this expression doesn't mean we've earned or deserve anything either. It simply stands as a marker of full commitment, much like a wedding vow. For a married couple, their wedding day wasn't the day they first fell in love with their spouse. But it *was* the day they celebrate as marking their *all-in commitment* to one another. There are many different ideas surrounding baptism, but let's allow God's Word to speak for itself.

[Christian Baptism]

Know Truth

Throughout this lesson, we're going to keep coming back to a common theme:
It honors God to *discover* what His Word teaches and *adjust to* that.

We'll specifically apply this to our topic of baptism. But if we start with assumptions about baptism — before we even look at the evidence— that's going to muddy our ability to discover what the passages are saying. We don't want to just assume that what *people* say about baptism is what *the Bible* actually says. Our goal is to discover and adjust. So let's start by clearing a few common biases.

I. Clearing Biases

A) Definition of Baptism

Some churches believe baptism can be applied by *various* methods, and others believe baptism refers to a *specific* method. So what would the original audience of the New Testament have understood the word "baptize" to mean?

As we covered in Lesson 1, the New Testament was originally written in Greek. And there were specific Greek verbs to convey the ideas of:

> pouring over — **καταχέω** (katacheo),
> sprinkling — **ῥαντίζω** (hrantizo), and even
> applying water by any method — **ὑδραίνω** (hudraino).

But even though some church traditions suggest these as different ways to be baptized, God didn't use any of those verbs to represent the idea of baptism in the New Testament. (He didn't even use that third, "just-get-'em-wet" word in the Bible — even though it was used in other ancient Greek writings, such as Homer's *Odyssey*.[1])

Instead, God used some form of the Greek verb **βαπτίζω** (baptizo) or the noun **βάπτισμα** (baptisma) in the New Testament 100 times! Our English word *baptize* came from this Greek word βαπτίζω (baptizo). So saying that *baptizo* means *baptize* is actually kind of circular — it doesn't really explain what that *means!*

According to Liddell and Scott's Greek dictionary[2] (called a "lexicon"), *baptizo* means to dip or plunge. According to Thayer's lexicon,[3] *baptizo* means to dip, immerse, submerge, wash, or overwhelm.

So when we look up the original meaning of the word, it becomes clear…

The original audience of the New Testament would have understood the word *baptize* to mean *immerse*.

So *by definition*, baptism is talking about immersion! This is a key insight that will help us avoid bringing presumptions into the Bible text. Remember, **it honors God to *discover* what His Word teaches and *adjust to* that.**

B) Types of Baptism?

Did God have *multiple ideas* in mind for Christian baptism? In particular, do some verses merely refer to a "physical (water) baptism" while others refer to a "spiritual baptism?" And if so, how would we differentiate between those for a particular passage?

Eph 4.4-6 (ESV) *There is one body and one Spirit—just as you were called to the one hope that belongs to your call—* ⁵ *one Lord, one faith, one baptism,* ⁶ *one God and Father of all, who is over all and through all and in all.*

The context shows that we're talking about *Christian* baptism here, not some other use of the word for *immerse*. So God answers our question quite clearly in v5. **There is *one* Christian baptism!** This verse would make no sense if there were actually separate physical and spiritual baptisms.

The implications of this are significant! It means that whenever we compare passages about Christian baptism, we don't have to sort out which kind of baptism they're talking about (physical or spiritual). Our understanding should not be "either/or," but rather "both/and," since there is *one* Christian baptism! This is an important concept to carry into the rest of our study.

It's also important to recognize whether the Bible spoke of other "baptisms" besides *Christian* baptism.

Read Acts 19.1-6.

Did people baptized by John still need to be baptized into Christ?

So was the baptism of John the same as or different from Christian baptism?

John the Baptist isn't around anymore, so why should this distinction *matter* to us? Well, since the Bible tells us the *history* of John's baptism, we should take care not to make assumptions about *Christian* baptism when we're actually reading passages about *John's* baptism.

So the Bible speaks of one Christian baptism, by immersion. And that one baptism is *different from* its predecessor, John's baptism. Again, **it honors God to *discover* what His Word teaches and *adjust to* that.**

C) Isn't Baptism a "Work?"

One last bias to consider is a big assumption that baptism could *not possibly be* connected with our commitment to Jesus because we're saved by grace.

Read Eph 2.8-9.

This passage talks about grace versus works, but it doesn't actually say *anything* about baptism. So for those who presume that baptism is a work — that idea either came from *another passage* in the Bible, *or* it came from a source *outside* the Bible.

The idea actually came from a 16th-century theologian named Huldreich Zwingli. He claimed that our salvation cannot have anything to do with something we do. His *presumption* was that since baptism is something we *do*, if we put that in the context of salvation, it must be a vain "work" opposed to God's grace.

But Zwingli's view was *different* from 1500 years of Christians who came before him! He even had the ego to claim, "in this matter of baptism, all the [teachers] have been in error from the time of the apostles."[4]

But the Bible does *not* equate false "works" with "doing," as Zwingli asserted. Rather, the Bible equates "works" (in the negative sense) with attempts at "earning" our salvation.

Read Rom 4.4 & 6.23.

The biblical idea of *grace* is that it's a free, undeserved *gift*. So the logical contrast between "grace" and "works" is the same as the contrast between "gift" and "wage." It's talking about *free* versus *earned*.

The truth Zwingli failed to recognize is that gifts need to be *received* — which requires some sort of "doing" step. Imagine you were given a coupon for a free beverage at Starbucks. • Once you know about the offer, you can either redeem that offer or not. (But simply believing the offer is valid doesn't put a drink in your hand!) If you redeem it, you're doing nothing to *pay for* it from your own earnings — it was a free gift. Yet you *"do" something to respond* to the offer by presenting the coupon to the cashier when you order. So...

Grace is *opposed to earning*, but actually <u>supported by</u> *responding* with action!

We're *not* saying at this point whether God intended baptism to be connected in some way to salvation or not. We're just saying the idea that baptism lines up more with *works* than *grace* — wasn't a *biblical* idea.

So now that we've addressed what the Bible *doesn't say* about the topic, let's allow God's Word speak for itself. Remember, **It honors God to *discover* what His Word teaches and *adjust to* that.**

II. What does the Bible teach about Christian baptism?

Remember, this is just our discovery step...

Acts 2.37-39 (ESV) *Now when they heard this they were cut to the heart, and said to Peter and the rest of the apostles, "Brothers, what shall we do?"* [38] *And Peter said to them, "Repent and be baptized every one of you in the name of Jesus Christ for the forgiveness of your sins, and you will receive the gift of the Holy Spirit.* [39] *For the promise is for you and for your children and for all who are far off, everyone whom the Lord our God calls to himself."*

According to v38, what are the two results of repenting and being baptized? (Circle in the text where you see those answers.)

Acts 22.14-16 (NAS) *"And he said, 'The God of our fathers has appointed you to know His will and to see the Righteous One and to hear an utterance from His mouth. [15] 'For you will be a witness for Him to all men of what you have seen and heard. [16] 'Now why do you delay? Get up and be baptized, and wash away your sins, calling on His name.'*

According to v16, what happens with our sins when we are baptized and call on His name? (Circle in the text where you see that answer.)

Verse 16 also said, "why do you delay?" Does that communicate a sense of urgency for baptism?

1Pet 3.18-22 (NIV) *For Christ also suffered once for sins, the righteous for the unrighteous, to bring you to God. He was put to death in the body but made alive in the Spirit. [19] After being made alive, he went and made proclamation to the imprisoned spirits— [20] to those who were disobedient long ago when God waited patiently in the days of Noah while the ark was being built. In it only a few people, eight in all, were saved through water, [21] and this water symbolizes baptism that now saves you also— not the removal of dirt from the body but the pledge of a clear conscience toward God. It saves you by the resurrection of Jesus Christ, [22] who has gone into heaven and is at God's right hand—with angels, authorities and powers in submission to him.*

What does v21 say it is that "saves" us — *by* **the power of Christ's resurrection, and as our (all-in) pledge to God?** (Circle the answer.)

Acts 8.35-39 (NIV) *Then Philip began with that very passage of Scripture and told him the good news about Jesus. [36] As they traveled along the road, they came to some water and the eunuch said, "Look, here is water. What can stand in the way of my being baptized?" [38] And he gave orders to stop the chariot. Then both Philip and the eunuch went down into the water and Philip baptized him. [39] When they came up out of the water, the Spirit of the Lord suddenly took Philip away, and the eunuch did not see him again, but went on his way rejoicing.*

Verse 35 said that Philip shared the Gospel (good news) with the eunuch. What was the eunuch's *response* **to hearing that good news?** (Circle the answer.)

Does the one Christian baptism involve water? (Circle the answer.)

Rom 6.3-8 (ESV) *Do you not know that all of us who have been baptized into Christ Jesus were baptized into his death? [4] We were buried therefore with him by baptism into death, in order that, just as Christ was raised from the dead by the glory of the Father, we too might walk in newness of life. [5] For if we have been united with him in a death like his, we shall certainly be united with him in a resurrection like his. [6] We know that our old self was crucified with him in order that the body of sin might be brought to nothing, so that we would no longer be enslaved to sin. [7] For one who has died has been set free from sin. [8] Now if we have died with Christ, we believe that we will also live with him.*

In v4-5, when were we united with Christ in His burial and resurrection?

What was symbolically crucified at that point (v6)? (Circle the answer.)

What did we *rise to* walk in (v4)? (Circle the answer.)

Matt 28.18-20 (ESV) *And Jesus came and said to them, "All authority in heaven and on earth has been given to me. ¹⁹ Go therefore and make disciples of all nations, baptizing them in the name of the Father and of the Son and of the Holy Spirit, ²⁰ teaching them to observe all that I have commanded you. And behold, I am with you always, to the end of the age."*

This was the mission that the resurrected Jesus charged His followers with. **Does our mission to "make disciples" involve baptizing people?**

1Cor 12.12-13 (NAS) *For even as the body is one and yet has many members, and all the members of the body, though they are many, are one body, so also is Christ. ¹³ For by one Spirit we were all baptized into one body, whether Jews or Greeks, whether slaves or free, and we were all made to drink of one Spirit.*

At what occasion did the Spirit connect us into the body of Christ (v13)?

Gal 3.26-27 (HCSB) *for you are all sons of God through faith in Christ Jesus. ²⁷ For as many of you as have been baptized into Christ have put on Christ like a garment.*

How many people have been clothed (covered) with Christ? (Circle the answer.)

 Process Truth

Remember the goal here is not to lead toward a particular doctrine. As followers of Jesus, our allegiance should always be to God and His Word — far above our loyalty to any particular brand of church. So, **it honors God to *discover* what His Word teaches and *adjust to* that.** So let's process what we've discovered.

Did the Clearing Biases section reveal any presumptions that you may have otherwise carried into the Bible text? If so, which ones?

Did the passages about Christian baptism reveal any new or different concepts to you? If so, what were the biggest ideas?

Apply Truth

So now comes the *adjusting* part…

Kyle Idleman made this observation from both Jesus' encounter with the woman at the well, and from his own pastoral experience: "I've learned that when someone is especially determined to talk about religion, it's often because they are desperately trying to keep Jesus from getting too personal."[5]

When Jesus brought up something about her personal life, the woman at the well immediately tried to turn the conversation into a religious debate: "Which mountain is the correct place to worship at?"

But Jesus brought it back to simply *pursuing God* since He is pursuing us (**John 4.19-24**)! Likewise for us, it's all about pursuing God; it's about worshiping Him in spirit and truth! **It honors God to *discover* what His Word teaches and *adjust to* that.**

We're saved by God's grace through faith, not by works — just like we read earlier in **Eph 2.8-9**! And we also just read several passages that put baptism directly in the context of going down into and up out of water, responding to the good news, demonstrating faith, repenting, calling on Jesus, being saved, being forgiven, receiving the Holy Spirit, being united with both Christ and the church, dying to our old self, receiving new life, etc! And we can be certain that all of that describes the "one baptism" that **Eph 4.5** talks about.

So if this discovery challenges our previous understanding of baptism, how do we respond to that in worship? How do we adjust to God's Word? How do we celebrate and embrace God's grace instead of trying to get technical and search for distractions or loopholes?[6]

Just like with the woman at the well,
Jesus is always more concerned with our present and future than our past!

There was a man in the New Testament who had a pretty impressive resume as a church leader — yet he had not been baptized into Christ. So when he finally learned about baptism, if anyone had incentives to blow religious smokescreens, it was probably this guy. His name was Apollos.

Acts 18.24-28 (ESV) *Now a Jew named Apollos, a native of Alexandria, came to Ephesus. He was an eloquent man, competent in the Scriptures.* [25] *He had been instructed in the way of the Lord. And being fervent in spirit, he spoke and taught accurately the things concerning Jesus, though he knew only the baptism of John.* [26] *He began to speak boldly in the synagogue, but when Priscilla and Aquila heard*

him, they took him aside and explained to him the way of God more accurately.²⁷ And when he wished to cross to Achaia, the brothers encouraged him and wrote to the disciples to welcome him. When he arrived, he greatly helped those who through grace had believed, ²⁸ for he powerfully refuted the Jews in public, showing by the Scriptures that the Christ was Jesus.

Here's that resume we can pull from the text. Apollos knew Scripture well (Old Testament prophecies about the Messiah). He'd been taught about Jesus ("the Lord"). He'd demonstrated repentance through John's baptism. He was a leader who preached about Jesus — accurately, passionately, boldly, and even eloquently. That's a pretty impressive list!

His one shortcoming was that he'd "*only*" experienced the baptism of John the Baptist (and not *Christian* baptism). So when Priscilla and Aquila realized this about Apollos, they took him aside and explained what he'd missed. The clear insinuation is that Apollos adjusted to this by getting baptized, because it took his ministry to the next level. Verses 27-28 added "great help" and "powerful" speaking to his resume.

While this was happening with Apollos, Paul also encountered a group of believers who didn't know about Christian baptism either. (We already looked at that passage in **Acts 19.1-6**.) But when these believers learned about baptism, they immediately followed through! Even though they had "technically" been "baptized" (though by John's baptism, not the one Christian baptism), they responded in worship. They embraced whatever they could do to help draw them closer to Jesus and to experience His Spirit in their lives.

And speaking of the Holy Spirit, an interesting thing happened to the first group of Gentiles who heard the Gospel message…

Acts 10.44-48 (ESV) *While Peter was still saying these things, the Holy Spirit fell on all who heard the word. ⁴⁵ And the believers from among the circumcised who had come with Peter were amazed, because the gift of the Holy Spirit was poured out even on the Gentiles. ⁴⁶ For they were hearing them speaking in tongues and extolling God. Then Peter declared, ⁴⁷ "Can anyone withhold water for baptizing these people, who have received the Holy Spirit just as we have?" ⁴⁸ And he commanded them to be baptized in the name of Jesus Christ. Then they asked him to remain for some days.*

These were the first people with no Jewish heritage to ever hear the Gospel message. And they *immediately* received the gift of the Holy Spirit! It was almost like the Spirit interrupted Peter's presentation of the Gospel! (This was the only time the Bible records it happening like this.) Yet even though Peter was the one who said in **Acts 2.38** that we'd receive the gift of the Holy Spirit once we repent are are baptized — Peter tells these Spirit-filled Gentiles to still be baptized. An argument *might* have been made that since they already had the Spirit, they didn't "need" to be baptized. But whether they needed it or not wasn't the issue. The issue was doing whatever they could to respond to and celebrate God's grace!

In all 3 of these examples, when the people *discovered* God's message about baptism, they *adjusted to* it. They responded! They rejoiced! And God was honored!

Consider again the illustration of a wedding. No one on their wedding day would make an issue about whether or not they "have to" exchange vows to be married before God. Instead, if they love their fiancé(e), they'd do *anything they can* to express that love and demonstrate their all-in commitment. Baptism is a lot like that wedding vow! Whether or not it's "essential" isn't the point.

The point is whether I'm willing to demonstrate my all-in commitment to Jesus, submit to His Lordship, and celebrate His grace! That's what it all boils down to.

Again, **Jesus is always more concerned with our present and future than our past!**

So what is the obvious application for anyone who desires to follow God but has not yet been immersed into Christ?

Have *you* done this?
> **If so, tell us a little about that.**
> **If not, what is your plan?** Remember that message of urgency in **Acts 22.16**? The NIV puts that urgency like this, "What are you waiting for?..."

Share Truth

Here are some ways we can share this truth with others...

☐ **If you choose to be baptized, post about it publicly. Invite people personally to watch and celebrate with you!**

☐ **Make sure you include the response of baptism when you share the Gospel** (as in Lesson 2).

☐ **If someone understands the offer of the Gospel and has committed in their heart to follow Jesus, but you discover they haven't been immersed, ask them if they'd be willing to go through what the Bible teaches about it.** (Like Priscilla and Aquila did with Apollos — it's that process of discovering and adjusting!)

☐ **Make sure your language is clear.** We don't ever need to be "re-baptized" since there is "one baptism." But it's good to make sure we've experienced that one baptism the way the Bible describes it (immersion as our own response to Jesus' offer of grace).

☐ **Be careful to communicate grace (and not judgment) as you share about this topic!** Don't let it become about rules, doctrines, have to's, or excuses — but about discovery and an opportunity to submit to our Lord and celebrate a clear demonstration of being all-in for Jesus!

 **Pray**

Thank God for being able to discover what His Word teaches about baptism. Thank Him for His wonderful offer of grace, and that He gave us a very tangible way to respond to it! Ask for courage and peace to take action if any "adjusting" still needs to happen.

1 Henry George Liddell, Robert Scott; revised by Sir Henry Stuart Jones and Roderick McKenzie, "ὑδραίνω entry," *A Greek-English Lexicon*. (Oxford; Oxford University Press Inc., 1843, 1845, 1849, 1855, 1861, 1869, 1882, 1897, 1940, 1996) 1844.

2 Henry George Liddell, Robert Scott; revised by Sir Henry Stuart Jones and Roderick McKenzie, "βαπτίζω entry," *A Greek-English Lexicon*. (Oxford; Oxford University Press Inc., 1843, 1845, 1849, 1855, 1861, 1869, 1882, 1897, 1940, 1996) 305.

3 Joseph Henry Thayer, "βαπτίζω entry," *A Greek–English Lexicon of the New Testament*. (New York; Harper & Brothers, 1889).

4 Jack Cottrell, *Set Free: What the Bible Says About Grace*, (Joplin, MO; College Press Publishing Company, 2010) 250-272.

5 Kyle Idleman, *Grace is Greater* (Grand Rapids, MI; BakerBooks, 2017) 44.

6 Many people think of the thief on the cross as a potential loophole. He didn't get baptized! However, the church (and therefore Christianity) began the day God poured out the Holy Spirit on the followers of Jesus. The thief on the cross died more than a month and a half before that! So he entered Paradise by way of the *Old Covenant*, trusting in the promised Messiah — who happened to be on the cross next to him. Instead of trying to come up with reasons not to be baptized, let's continue in the reading to look at 3 examples of people who said "why not?"

Made in the USA
Lexington, KY
11 December 2018